# Intuitive Security
# for Women

# Intuitive Security
# for Women

by Lloyd Vaughan with Luke Chao

BURMANBOOKS
.com

Published by BurmanBooks Inc.
4 Lamay Cres. Scarborough, Ontario Canada M1X 1J1

**BURMAN**BOOKS
.com

Vaughan, Lloyd
The Inner Power Series for Intuitive Security for Women /
Lloyd Vaughan

Cover Design by www.AliveDesign.com

Edited by Solidus Communications www.solidus.ca

Typesetting by TypeWorx

Distribution:

Canada: Jaguar Book Group;
100 Armstrong Avenue
Georgetown, Ontario L7G 5S4

United States: Independent Publishers Group,
814 North Franklin Street,
Chicago, Ill 60610

ISBN 0-9736632-8-6

For Abby, Shelby, Alyssa, Makenna,
Brooke, Tanner, Muriel, and Lillian.

# A letter from the publisher

Dear Valued Reader;

The idea of The Inner Power Series came about after I spent some years in the film industry making movies like *Spider* with David Cronenberg, and TV shows like *Sidebar* on CBC Newsworld all by the time I was twenty-eight years of age. I decided to take some time off from the entertainment industry, since the more I accomplished the less happy I became.

Fate drew me to the authors who eventually wrote The Inner Power Series books. They were all very accomplished professionals who seemed to really enjoy life, earn great livings and yet stay grounded. Their stories, philosophies and accomplishments in helping other people inspired me to start the company and launch these books.

I knew I was on the right track, since all the other publishers turned me down (which generally is a great sign!), and from envisioning one that led to five in only four months, we have put together this special series.

I know you will notice the difference immediately after reading and learning the best techniques from the best teachers. We look forward to being your partners during your inner growth period. We want to help you accomplish your goals and achieve the greatness that is within you. Please write to us and let us know about your experiences after reading this book.

Yours truly,

Sanjay Burman
BurmanBooks Inc.

BurmanBooks.com

## Acknowledgements

With thanks to
Luke Chao,
for his writing skills and intuitive insight,
Sanjay Burman,
without whom this book would not have been possible
and all the women
whose stories are told in this book.

Special thanks go to my business partner
Tyrone (Ty) Watts
at LTD & Associates Inc.,
for his ongoing support in all our endeavors.

# Table of Contents

Page

# Preface

In preparation for writing this book, I conducted the usual research by reading newspaper and magazine articles, spending countless hours surfing the Internet compiling mounds of information, and recalling my own experiences and knowledge. However, it was when I reached out to women of all ages for their stories, thoughts and ideas on personal safety that it all came together.

I'm grateful to them for sharing their accounts. When you read this book, you too will come to appreciate the contributions they've made, as it's you, the reader, they're reaching out to.

If you're looking for information on physical defense, this isn't the book for you. But if you want to learn from others—your peers—describing the difficult situations they've found themselves in, how they felt, how they dealt with it and what you can learn from their experience, read on.

You'll also learn how some crimes are committed and what you can do to avoid or minimize their effect on you and your loved ones.

Although this book was written with women in mind, every chapter has advice that can benefit men—even the chapter on stalking, in which I share my personal experience with you.

The common theme throughout this book, the book's goal, is to help you become Alert and Intrepid.

# Chapter 1:
# The Importance of Being Vigilant

Driving down a rural Ontario road one afternoon, Lauren noticed flashing lights in her rear-view mirror. They looked like police lights, but the car following her was unmarked—a discrepancy that made her suspicious. Still, she was concerned. Could she have made an illegal maneuver without realizing it?

Lauren had been taught never to pull over for an unmarked car, so she used her cell phone to dial *677, the number for the Ontario Provincial Police. She told the dispatcher that there was a car with flashing lights following her, but that she didn't want to pull over until the dispatcher verified that it was a legitimate police car.

This action may have saved her life. The dispatcher checked to see if there were police cars in the area and came up empty. He told Lauren to continue driving and that help was on its way.

Ten minutes later, police cruisers stopped and surrounded both cars. One officer approached Lauren, while other officers surrounded the pursuer's car. After a brief struggle, Lauren's pursuer was in police custody.

The man was a convicted rapist and a wanted criminal.


There's a reason you picked up this book. Maybe you've heard about increased violence in our cities. Maybe your house has been broken into or maybe one of your friends has been assaulted. Or maybe you just felt drawn to the topic of personal safety for some reason you can't explain. Regardless of why you picked up this book, you've made a decision to become more aware of crime and your personal security. This alone gives you an advantage over most women in North America.

In Lauren's story, Lauren took quick action to protect herself from danger, despite pressure from someone pretending to be an authority. In more than one case, a rapist has impersonated a police officer to commit his crime. When this disguise has failed, it's often because his target refused to accept it at face value. As you'll discover, many crimes are possible only because the victims accept the masks of criminals without question, even when there are hints that something's wrong. You'll learn to become more aware of criminals in disguise and to listen to your inner voice when it warns of danger. That's what Lauren did, and she'll never regret it.

To help you get the most out of this book, below, make a list of the positive goals you'll achieve by becoming more aware of your personal security. Write down all the things you want— *not* the things you *don't* want. For example, "I don't want to die," is a negative goal. If this is your goal, write instead, "I want to live and watch my family grow, in safety and comfort." Now write out your goals, as many as you can think of, and read this book with those goals in mind. That way, you'll get precisely what you want.

## My Goals in Achieving Greater Personal Security

1) _____

2) _____

3) _____

4) _____

5) _____

## Alert and Intrepid is the most secure attitude

A woman's response to a dangerous situation is usually dependent on two factors: how threatened she feels and how empowered she feels to respond to the threat. These two factors combine to describe the three main attitudes a person can have to a given situation:

1) **Sleepwalking:** Someone who's sleepwalking through a situation is living inside her own head, oblivious to the potential dangers around her. In many cases, she's preoccupied with work or home responsibilities—perfectly good priorities, but not when they preclude attention to safety. When alerted to potential risks, she typically responds, "I never thought about that before!"

2) **Captivated by fear:** Someone who's captivated by fear is afraid to venture out. Even when she's alone in her own home, she's anxious. Because she's terrified of dangers, real or imagined, she can't enjoy life fully. Her mantra is, "Do you know what could happen?"

3) **Alert and Intrepid:** Someone who's Alert and Intrepid is aware of potential risks, knows how to protect herself and can react appropriately if faced with a real threat. That means she can stride through life confidently, enjoying it to full advantage.

In other words, if you're oblivious to the dangers of a situation, regardless of whether or not you can protect yourself, you'll probably exhibit sleepwalking behaviors. If you're aware of the danger, but don't feel equipped to protect yourself, it's almost instinctual to exhibit captivated by fear behaviors. But if you're fully aware of the dangers and you *do* feel equipped to protect yourself, you're most likely to exhibit Alert and Intrepid behaviors.

Personally, I'm biased toward the last category. Women should be Alert to danger and Intrepid about the world around them. I hope you agree.

Some women don't want to raise their awareness of crime, because they believe it leads to a captivated by fear attitude. But this doesn't have to be the case. There's a distinction between being captivated by fear and being Alert and Intrepid. Someone who's captivated by fear is focused on what *could* happen, while someone who's Alert and Intrepid is focused on what's *actually* happening. Sure, a woman who's Alert and Intrepid is aware of what could happen, but she uses that knowledge to inform her observations of the world around her. The woman who's sleep-walking or captivated by fear is too focused on what's happening inside her own head to know what's happening in her vicinity. When you're Alert and Intrepid, you're focused on the world itself; you feel so confident in yourself that knowledge of crime doesn't stop you from doing what you want to do in life.

In his studies on personality, Dr. John M. Oldham identified six traits of the Vigilant personality type, a good model for the Alert and Intrepid woman. These traits are 1) autonomy, 2) caution, 3) perceptiveness, 4) self-defensiveness, 5) alertness to criticism and 6) fidelity. Those who have a Vigilant-style personality can take care of themselves and don't require the assurance or approval of others. They're careful of whom they deal with and how they deal with them; they're good listeners who consider every aspect of communication, not only language.

When they have to stand up for themselves, they do so quickly and decisively. Although much of personality is innate, consider how you could emulate these behaviors and strengthen them in yourself.

## Self-assessment

Please read each of the situations below and consider how you tend to react in them. Then tick the appropriate column. Be honest with yourself; no one has to see your answers. If an experience doesn't apply to you, move to the next situation.

| Situation | Sleepwalking | Captivated by fear | Alert and Intrepid |
|---|---|---|---|
| Being at home alone | ❑ | ❑ | ❑ |
| Answering your door or telephone | ❑ | ❑ | ❑ |
| Opening your mail | ❑ | ❑ | ❑ |
| Walking or jogging in your neighborhood | ❑ | ❑ | ❑ |
| Driving | ❑ | ❑ | ❑ |
| Shopping | ❑ | ❑ | ❑ |
| Living or working in a high-rise building | ❑ | ❑ | ❑ |
| Working late | ❑ | ❑ | ❑ |
| Guarding your computer and Internet privacy | ❑ | ❑ | ❑ |
| Preventing identity theft | ❑ | ❑ | ❑ |
| Traveling in North America | ❑ | ❑ | ❑ |
| Traveling outside North America | ❑ | ❑ | ❑ |

Your results in this assessment can help you refine your goals for reading this book, since any checkmarks in the first two columns present areas for improvement. Pay particular attention to the chapters dealing with these situations. In a few weeks' time, consider reviewing this assessment to see how much you've improved.

## Crime: what, who and when

Let's take a brief look at some statistics. Violent crimes such as homicide, assault and robbery get most of the attention, but they account for less than fifteen percent of all crimes reported in North America. Crimes such as fraud, theft, and breaking and entering account for over half of all crimes committed.

People with the lowest income report the highest incidence of violent crime, while those with the highest income report the highest incidence of property crime. Household crime is highest for those living in duplex, semi-detached or row houses, and lower in apartments and single dwellings. The highest rate of violent crime occurs at night, between six p.m. and midnight, peaking annually in the summertime. Thefts are generally committed between noon and six p.m. In both rural and urban areas, people with the highest victimization rates include women, youths, single people and students. Social values, lifestyle and socio-economic status also affect victimization rates.

Of course, these are just statistics. The goal of this book is to help you avoid becoming one.

Jackie was struggling to lift heavy groceries into the trunk of her car, when a young man stopped to offer help.

"Thanks," Jackie panted, giving him a glance, "but I'm all right." In truth, she wasn't; she really did need help. However, she'd once accepted unsolicited help from a stranger and after-wards he wouldn't leave her alone. She got the impression that he wasn't really helping her; he was helping himself *to* her. After this experience, she decided it was easier to do her own heavy lifting.

"You don't look all right," the young man said. He grabbed a bag of potatoes and heaved it into her trunk.

"Let go of my groceries!" Jackie said suddenly. Something about this young man reminded her of the previous stranger. She felt an unpleasant sensation throughout her entire body.

He ignored her, grabbing the same grocery bag as Jackie did. They wrestled over it briefly.

"Let *go*!" said Jackie.

"Lady," the young man said, "I'm just trying to help."

"And I thank you," Jackie said, straightening her back and looking as fierce as she could. "The best way you can help me is by letting me finish loading my groceries by myself. You're making me uncomfortable. You can help me by continuing on your way—*please*."

The young man scowled, but he couldn't think of a response. "Fine," he said angrily and stormed away.

With adrenaline coursing through her bloodstream, Jackie finished loading the groceries into her car at record speed and hurriedly drove away.


While it's true that the young man might have been a genuinely helpful individual with poor social skills, it's also true that a person who's pushy to offer help will likely be pushy after-wards. Jackie let experience inform her behavior and took the action she thought was appropriate. But did she actually prevent a rape or carjacking? There would have been only one way for her to find out, and Jackie chose not to take it.

## Nothing guarantees the prevention of crime, but precautions can help

There are three causes of random violence:
1) Lack of awareness.
2) Body language.
3) Being in the wrong place at the wrong time.

We'll address awareness of crime throughout this book.

Timid body language looks like a bull's eye to an attacker. Anywhere you go, look like you belong there. Keep your head up and stride confidently. We'll discuss confidence and body language in more detail in the next two chapters.

As for completely random violence, there's always the possibility it could happen. You can reduce your risks by using the techniques presented in this book.

However, most violence isn't perpetrated randomly by strangers, but by those you know. While no one wants to be constantly on guard around friends and family, and while it's often hardest to defend against those closest to you, sometimes you have to.

Some women are reluctant to use defensive tactics even with strangers, because they think it's impolite. Remember that anyone who truly has your best interests in mind will accept your concerns and leave you alone. Someone who calls you names after you've crossed the street to avoid them is precisely the type of individual you *should* be avoiding! Acting in your own defense won't turn a non-violent person criminal.

Self-defense doesn't mean learning how to fight, which in some situations may even get you hurt. Self-defense is essentially about your frame of mind. It means avoiding potentially dangerous situations and being alert to your surroundings. It means being aware of escape routes and communicating assertively with those you're forced to interact with.

Taking a self-defense class can add to your defensive skills. Make sure the course you select teaches self-defense specifically, rather than martial arts. While proficiency in martial arts can help, most martial arts place too much emphasis on a fair fight and they take years to master. Meanwhile, they'll instill in you just enough confidence that you stay and fight, rather than running away.

On the street, there are no fair fights. In fact, an attacker will target you specifically because he thinks he can readily take advantage of you. When you have a serious disadvantage in size, strength and experience, the best course of action is to run away and the second best is to fight dirty. You can't learn to play the violin just by reading about it, and the only way to become skilled at physical self-defense is through practice and learning from a good self-defense course.

Earlier, I asked you to define your goals in reading this book. These are my goals in writing it:
1) So you can avoid being a victim of crime.
2) So you can become aware of risks and equipped to protect yourself from them.
3) So you can live your life to the fullest, while being alert to danger, but not held hostage by fear.

The advice in this book is based on research, training and decades of experience in law enforcement and personal security.

However, I can't tell you precisely what to do, because every situation is different. Instead, think of my advice as increasing your range of choices. The more choices you have, the more flexibility you have when responding to situations. Even though that doesn't *guarantee* your safety, it's much better than being unprepared.

## Summary

Nothing you do can totally guarantee your safety. But everything you do to protect yourself empowers you to live your life. Become aware of your sleepwalking or captivated by fear behaviors and resolve to be Alert and Intrepid.

The keys to self-defense are awareness and mental preparation. In the next chapter, we'll talk about the mental game.

# Chapter 2:
# The Mental Game

On weekends, Julia painted portraits. At first, she painted them for her friends and family without charge, but it wasn't long before she discovered that she had talent. With her friends' encouragement, she set up a small studio in her basement. She'd practice hard and once she was confident in her ability, she'd start charging for commissioned portraits.

The more Julia practiced, the more she noticed the faces around her. Everywhere she went, she scrutinized faces for their proportions, colors, imperfections and expressions. Before long, she couldn't stop analyzing the faces she saw even if she wanted to. As automatically as she recognized her own mother, she could study and reproduce any face she'd observed.

Julia's other hobby was jogging. Every weekday morning, she woke up at six a.m. for a quick run along the local trails. It wasn't long before she came to know the regulars, and after she started painting portraits, even strange faces weren't strange for long.

Julia made a game of it. Whenever she saw a jogger approaching from a distance, she tried to guess the jogger's identity. As they came closer and she could see the other jogger more clearly, she'd either award or deduct points for getting the identity right or wrong. If she didn't recognize a face, she made an effort to analyze it, remembering its features and proportions, as though she were going to paint it.

One day, police issued a bulletin seeking information on a man who'd tried to attack a jogger in the park. Julia had been on the trails that morning, so she tried to think of all the faces she'd passed on the trail. There was only one stranger and she remembered his facial features in fine detail.

Julia painted his portrait and gave it to the police, who were surprised, but grateful. With the victim's description of the attacker and a matching portrait in hand, the police were able to apprehend the suspect quickly.

Word of the unusual case spread rapidly and Julia's portrait studio made a profit in its first month of business.

## Awareness is key

At any given moment, your attention can be focused inward or outward. If you're daydreaming, reflecting on the day's events or worrying about the future, your attention is focused inward. Reflection and planning are useful at times, but not on the street. This is the typical sleepwalker profile: the eyes are open, but the mind is somewhere else. Another example of inward-focused attention is being captivated by fear or any emotion. By definition, any time your attention is focused inside your own head, it's facing away from the world around you.

When you're Alert and Intrepid, your attention is focused outward. You still have thoughts and emotions, but these are secondary to what you're aware of through your eyes and ears. You're living in the present moment. If anything seems amiss, you don't panic or wildly speculate about what might be going on. You observe the situation and react to it as it develops. In some ways, awareness is the opposite of fear. Fear is often a dread of the unknown; awareness is a way of seeing into the shadows. When you look at someone with all your attention focused on him, what you're saying is, "Yes, I know you're there and I'm already well ahead of you." That's the attitude of the Alert and Intrepid woman.

Everyone drifts between inward-facing and outward-facing attention from minute to minute. Awareness directed inward isn't inherently bad. When you're painting or writing, you benefit greatly from having a rich inner reality. When you're considering buying a house or making a financial investment, your analytical brain is rightly turned inward. When you're pondering life's big questions, you *want* to plumb the depths of your mind. It's useful in those contexts to have an inward focus, but it's useful when you're walking down the street or through a parking garage to have an outward focus.

The next time you're walking down the street, try this exercise. Begin by noticing the sights around you: the colors of buildings, styles of clothing people are wearing, the way close objects and distant objects intermesh as you move. Then allow your eyes to lose focus and view the world using your peripheral vision, which is much better at detecting movement than is our normally focused eyesight. Cease unnecessary thought and slow the chatter inside your mind—a process that will come naturally as you focus your attention outward. Then listen for sounds. Can you hear traffic, birds, voices, footsteps? Engage your curiosity by paying attention to those sounds and any sensations you feel. How does the ground feel beneath your feet? How does the wind feel on your face? Is it hot or cold? How does the air smell? How does it change as you walk down the street?

Once you're fully focused on the world around you, squeeze your left fist and inside your head, say, "Awareness!" or a similar keyword. Then focus your attention on each of your senses, one by one. As you do so, squeeze your left fist again and repeat your keyword. Once you've focused on each of your five senses, repeat the procedure to reinforce your mental link to that alert, outward-focused state.

Once you've established this link, if you find yourself drifting and want to bring yourself to a fully aware state quickly, squeeze your left fist and inside your head, say your keyword.

## Tune into your unconscious mind; allow your intuition to warn you of danger

We all have a conscious mind and an unconscious mind. Your conscious mind is what you're currently aware of, such as the words you're reading, your thoughts about them or aspects of the environment you're in. It's analytical, focused and usually verbal. If you can purposefully think something, it's in the conscious mind. On the evolutionary scale, the conscious mind is a fairly recent development, but the rapid growth of human intellect over the past few thousand years would have been impossible without it.

The unconscious mind, by definition, is everything outside the conscious mind. Human beings have had an unconscious mind for much longer than they've had a conscious mind. It controls instinct, emotion and bodily processes like breathing and digestion. Although it isn't as focused and logical as the conscious mind, it can quickly process *many* pieces of information simultaneously. For millions of years, it's evolved to help us survive in the world without thinking.

How does a mother know when her child is lying? We might call it "feminine intuition." Because she's spent so much time with her child, every nuance of his normal behavior and personality is embedded in her unconscious mind. When her child deviates from the norm, even slightly, she knows it immediately, not through analysis, but through a *feeling* that something's wrong. Even if she can't provide logical facts to justify that feeling, if she follows through on her hunch, she'll confirm that she's right.

In a similar way, your unconscious mind knows how a normal, trustworthy person behaves. If a stranger deviates from this behavior, the survival instinct of your unconscious mind will tell you—as long as you listen. Intuition isn't a mysterious, all-knowing power. It's simply a message from your unconscious mind that arrives as a "gut feeling" or a sensation of "just knowing" something. Everyone has a sense of intuition, but some people choose to ignore it because it isn't rational. And it's true: intuition is plainly irrational. But if you try to analyze your way out of rapidly escalating violence, you'll realize that in some cases, instinct is a much more effective tool than reason.

Some people don't hear their intuition at all, because their minds are too cluttered with other thoughts. Imagine your mind as a calm sea and intuition as a pebble dropped into it. If the sea's placid, the pebble will display perfect, concentric circles and you'll be able to pinpoint it at once. But if the sea's stormy, the pebble will be lost among the waves. To develop a calmer mind and finer-tuned intuition, keep your attention focused away from your everyday worries and toward your senses. The awareness exercise previously described in this chapter can help you achieve this. For intuition to work well, you need to quietly observe everything around you.

Let's say you think someone's lying. His words are saying one thing, his tone of voice is saying another and his body language is saying something else entirely. How much credence do we give each of these forms of communication?

According to a 1971 study by Albert Mehrabian of UCLA, when experimental subjects perceived that a speaker's messages didn't match up, they gave only seven percent of their credit to the words, the conscious portion of communication. Body language and voice tone, the unconscious portions, accounted for fifty-five and thirty-eight percent of the communication, respectively.

For example, if a stranger's looming over you and growling, "I'm not gonna hurt you," which do you believe, his words or his body language? You don't have to think, "Well, he says he's not going to hurt me, but he's furrowing his brow and raising his hand, so I guess he's lying and maybe I should try to make an escape." No, you trust your intuition and run.

If you ever get an uncomfortable feeling that you're in danger, simply accept it. Trying to analyze it, or worse, trying to talk yourself out of being "irrational," is applying the wrong tool to the task. The conscious mind is like a laser, narrow and focused, while the unconscious mind is like a light bulb, wide and diffused. They serve entirely different purposes. A laser beam can cut through steel or perform delicate surgery, but you need a light bulb to illuminate the room you're working in. You can't illuminate a room with a laser and you can't analyze a situation through logic when you need to respond immediately.

## Learn to control your mental state

We can't always change the outside world, but we can change our response to it. We can change our beliefs, our feelings and our attitudes so that our inner selves are more powerful, forward-looking and capable.

Self-confidence comes from knowing you can cope with a given situation, and that wards off fear. Often, that's enough to prevent trouble. Fear is one of the primary weapons bullies and criminals use, because someone who's afraid can easily be controlled. If an attacker senses fear in a potential target, he's more likely to choose that person as his next victim. However, the reverse also holds true. Criminals can sense the absence of fear in a potential target and they're less likely to approach you if you're calm, confident and unafraid.

Think back to the awareness exercise we did earlier in this chapter and how it helped you become more aware of everything you see, hear and feel around you. Now let's do something similar for your self-confidence.

Think of something that raises your self-confidence. Imagine yourself playing the role of a favorite heroine, a childhood role model or a brave citizen you heard about on the news. Or perhaps you remember a time when you felt on top of the world; maybe you'd just talked down the schoolyard bully or finished a performance you felt proud of. Alternatively, try imagining yourself responding to a situation assertively and confidently in the future.

Let these confident feelings grow and spread throughout your entire body, from the top of your head to the bottoms of your feet. As the feelings build, squeeze your *right* hand into a fist and say inside your head, loudly and confidently, "Confidence!" Repeat this several times, thinking of different scenarios each time.

After completing this exercise, you can discreetly squeeze your right fist and say inside your head, "Confidence!" whenever you want to evoke that state. Try it. If it doesn't work initially, repeat the exercise, thinking of different scenarios.

This technique is called anchoring and once you've mastered it, you can use it to associate any emotional state to any "anchor." The anchor doesn't necessarily have to be a squeezed fist and a recited word. It can be any kind of sensory stimulation.

Sometimes, people inadvertently anchor emotions to an evocative photograph placed inside a locket or the scent of a cologne worn on a special night.

Play around with what makes you feel great about yourself. Then keep what works, and throw the rest away.

Melanie loved dogs. She bought her house specifically because it had a big backyard for her three German shepherds. They were friendly and loved playing with people, but sometimes they chased and killed small animals.

One day, Melanie's neighbor Denise knocked on her door, looking upset.

"Have you seen my rabbit?" Denise asked. "He's escaped."

"I haven't," Melanie said, "but I'll check my yard."

She invited Denise to follow and they walked to the back patio, where they saw the three dogs excitedly clustered around the deck. Denise let out a cry.

Melanie ran to her dogs and pulled them aside. "I think I found your rabbit," she said, reaching under the deck.

"Why don't you chain up those *beasts*?" Denise demanded.

Melanie ignored her and examined the rabbit. "He doesn't look hurt. Just a little shocked. Here, take a look."

Denise grabbed the rabbit from Melanie's hands, cradled him in her arms and stroked him vigorously. "They should be put to sleep!"

"They're my dogs and I'm not putting them to sleep."

"Well, they *should* be! They're *vicious, monstrous, wild…*" Denise trailed off as she ran out of adjectives. By now, she was nearly in Melanie's face and her grip on the rabbit had tightened so much, he was squirming uncomfortably in her arms. "Beasts!" she spat.

"You're right," Melanie said without a trace of irony. "My dogs can be wild and vicious sometimes. They've even killed small animals. I agree that they should have been chained up when your rabbit was in my backyard. I'm happy to see they didn't hurt him."

"That's right," Denise said. She smiled awkwardly and turned to carry her rabbit home.

Melanie could have made a rational argument against Denise, but since Denise was so overcome by emotion, it likely wouldn't have worked. Nor would returning the anger have worked, since an argument could have ended with violence, or at least hypertension. Instead, she agreed to as much of what Denise had to say as she could, and left the rest unsaid.

## Everyone thinks he or she is right

Everyone's thoughts and actions, no matter how unreasonable or criminal, have some kind of internal logic. A stalker actually believes that if he calls you ten times a day, you might fall in love with him. A mugger might think that his broken childhood or the disparity between his poverty and your wealth, justifies his mugging you. You could argue against his internal logic, but in most cases, this is just as futile as him trying to convince you of his perspective.

Even if you can't accept his internal logic, try to make sense of it. Ignoring another person's view of the world provides false security, while understanding it can help you predict and respond to his behavior.

## Summary

Living life with greater awareness is living life more safely. Tune out mental distractions and develop a curiosity about the world around you. If you feel uncomfortable somewhere, trust your instincts and leave. Learn to control your own mental state and develop an understanding of other people, even criminals.

# Chapter 3:
# Street Smarts

On a Friday afternoon, Juliana entered a Toronto subway station. She was wearing clothing she thought was inconspicuous for a young university student, but a group of five teenage girls standing farther down the platform had another idea. As they looked at Juliana, one of them sang, "Money, money, money, money," the theme to Donald Trump's television show *The Apprentice*.

Juliana's stomach clenched, but she told herself that they couldn't possibly be directing their taunts toward her. She wasn't rich and it would be paranoid to think she was in danger on a crowded subway platform on a weekday afternoon.

Juliana should have trusted her intuition. For the next ten minutes, the group continued to harass her. Then, the girl who'd been chanting "money," who seemed to be the group's leader, stepped forward and purposefully bumped into Juliana. Juliana looked away and walked farther down the platform, but the group followed. The girl approached her again, pushed her and screamed "Boo!" Juliana ignored her and walked farther away.

When the girl pushed her once more, Juliana ran into a subway car, hoping she'd lost the group. She discovered she was wrong, when she felt another push from behind and heard another screamed word.

The girl asked Juliana where she got her "little Gucci purse"—actually a cheap imitation leather handbag. Even though the girl had one hand on her shoulder and another on the purse, Juliana ignored her. Several passengers watched the incident without intervening.

Finally, Juliana looked the girl in the eyes and said, "What do you have to do with me? Do you even know me? Leave me alone."

The girl screamed again. Juliana ran the length of the subway car and exited at a busy station. She started running up the stairs, but felt a tug at her purse pulling her down. It was the girl. Juliana pushed the hand away and ran back down to the platform. The girl followed, pushing Juliana with full force and knocking her to the ground. Then the girl ran away.

Juliana was hysterical. She got up from the ground, found a telephone and dialed her boyfriend. Another member of the group approached her, apologized and pleaded for her not to call the police. The new girl tried to hug Juliana and wanted her to accept an apology from the bullying friend. Juliana told her that she just wanted to be left alone.

Despite the taunts of "money," this attack wasn't motivated by profit. It was a case of a teenage bully having some sadistic fun at the expense of someone who seemed like a good victim. While the attack was definitely *not* Juliana's fault, there are some precautions she could have taken to make herself a less likely target. First, she didn't listen to her intuition, which immediately informed her that something was wrong. Second, she didn't assert herself soon enough. Ignoring a bully can sometimes work, but in other cases, it provokes the bully to escalate her attacks. Third, Juliana didn't make eye contact, another mark of a lack of assertiveness. Fourth, in all likelihood, Juliana showed fear, which the other girl played on by shouting "Boo!" Fear attracts bullies, just as assertiveness repels them. Finally, she'd expected other people to automatically come to her aid. If you want help, you have to ask for it, especially in a large crowd or a big city. It's too easy to find anonymity in a crowd.

## Stand confidently and walk purposefully

Although body language accounts for fifty-five percent of communication when you're talking to someone face-to-face, it accounts for *all* your communication when you're walking down the street. It's important to realize what your body, posture and manner of walking say about you.

In a 1981 study, Betty Grayson and Morris Stein videotaped pedestrians on the streets of New York City and showed the tapes to several prisoners convicted of violent crimes. They asked the prisoners to identify which pedestrians they'd most likely target as victims—which they did in seconds. To the researchers' surprise, they found that in most cases, the convicts selected the same victims. Moreover, they didn't always select the smallest or weakest-looking pedestrians, but sometimes chose full-grown men. When asked why they had selected those particular victims, in most cases, they couldn't give an explanation. They *just knew* who'd make an easy target and who'd fight back.

Grayson and Stein examined the videotapes to find characteristics common to the pedestrians identified as potential victims. They found that these people tended to walk with a longer or shorter stride than normal. They often dragged or shuffled their feet and they tended to shift their body weight from side to side when they moved. Overall, their body movements were awkward and uncoordinated. Their bodies seemed to move as a collection of independent parts, like a marionette, rather than as a unified whole. Non-victims, on the other hand, had a smoother stride, of a normal length. They moved with purpose and coordination, and their bodies seemed to move as a whole, from their center. Their posture was upright and they looked around as they walked.

Consider the characteristics of people identified by criminals as victims and non-victims. Which correspond to the sleepwalker or captivated by fear profile and which correspond to the Alert and Intrepid profile? Becoming more confident and more aware of your surroundings—mastering the mental game of being an Alert and Intrepid woman—will show in your body language.

The reverse is also true. Try this exercise. If you're slouching, sit up straight. If your eyes are downcast, turn your gaze forward, toward the horizon. If your face is blank, smile as broadly as you can and hold that smile for a few seconds. Doesn't that make you feel better? For most women, this revelation isn't a surprise: looking great makes you feel great.

If a stranger engages you in conversation on the street, maintain a confident poise. Keep your body and head erect. Maintain eye contact; avoid lowering your eyes and looking at the ground—this is a sign of submission. If eye contact makes you feel uncomfortable, look at his ear or nose, since it's unlikely he'll be able to tell the difference. Keep your voice firm and clear when you're speaking.

The only exception to maintaining eye contact is when you're passing a strange man on the street. Looking at him for longer than two or three seconds can be interpreted as sexual interest.

In most cases, projecting a confident attitude through body language will convince an attacker to move to an easier target. If you look alert and self-assured, and walk with a purposeful stride, few people will think they can take advantage of you readily.

## If you feel too passive, consider assertiveness training

Assertiveness is an cure for passivity, fear, shyness and even anger. Whenever "nice" people allow a dominant or greedy person to take advantage of them, they're reinforcing their aggressor's unfair, self-centered behavior, but they're also cheating themselves. This isn't being nice; it's being passive.

Many people recognize that they're being taken advantage of, but have difficulty saying no. An aggressive person will continue his behavior if it gives him positive results, so nothing changes unless a victim recognizes that her rights are being denied and she takes appropriate action. Keeping a diary of situations you find difficult, situations in which you feel you're being manipulated, may help you analyze their dynamics and provide useful information about what you could do differently. If you sometimes feel submissive, recognize the harm you could be doing to yourself by not learning to become more assertive. You might be cheating yourself out of something you deserve. You may suffer from diminished self-respect and lose the respect of others. By concealing your feelings, you're being dishonest with yourself and those around you.

Assertiveness tends to lead to greater happiness and self-respect. Are you comfortable stating your opinion, even when others disagree? Asserting yourself isn't always easy. Some people confuse assertiveness with aggressiveness and view it as a negative behavior. Even though people interchange the terms assertiveness and aggressiveness, they're not the same thing. *Webster's Revised Unabridged Dictionary* defines the two words very differently:

> **Assertive**   Positive; affirming confidently; affirmative; peremptory. In a confident and assertive form.

> **Aggressive** Tending or disposed to aggress;
> characterized by aggression; making assaults;
> unjustly attacking; as, an aggressive policy,
> war, person, nation.

Assertiveness is the ability to comfortably express what you think, feel and want. It's expressing a viewpoint or need without offending others and without anger or attack.

Aggressiveness, on the other hand, uses force and manipulative tactics and is usually at the expense of others.

Aggressiveness and assertiveness are like points on a spectrum, with passiveness on the far left, assertiveness in the middle and aggressiveness on the far right. Consider where you fit in this continuum by observing yourself in everyday situations. Do you find yourself acting the aggressor? Behaving as a rational, assertive adult? Submitting passively and timidly, even though it means you don't get what you deserve or desire? To feel best about yourself and gain the respect of others, aim to be in the middle of the continuum, a rational, assertive adult.

If you find it difficult to be assertive, practice positive self-talk and conscious assertive behavior. Leave old habits behind. You'll feel better about yourself, and much more Alert and Intrepid.

## Avoid danger

There's truth in the old adage that an ounce of prevention is worth a pound of cure. If you sense there might be danger, trust your instincts and avoid it. If an uncomfortable situation develops, leave. There are steps you can take to reduce your risk:

- Stay in well-lit, populated areas.
- Walk down the middle of the sidewalk, on the left side of the street, so you can see oncoming cars.

- Keep your distance from doorways, alley entrances, shrubbery, parked cars, and anywhere else a criminal might hide.
- If someone in a car stops to ask you for directions, maintain a safe distance from the vehicle. Never get close to or into the car.
- Avoid jogging or walking alone at night.
- Don't use headphones, since they greatly diminish your awareness of your surroundings.
- Have your keys ready when you approach your car or house.

If you think you're being followed or targeted, acknowledge your pursuer, then head toward a busy or populated area, like a neighbor's home, open business, police station or fire station. If you're not sure if you're in danger, but you have a mobile phone, call a friend, tell him or her where you are, and keep talking while remaining alert. This will often deter an attacker, who may suspect you're calling the police. If you are attacked, your friend will know immediately and can summon help. Keeping 911 on speed dial is another good idea. Even if you drop your phone or you're unable to talk to the dispatcher, emergency services in most cities can determine your location through the origin of your phone's signal.

Jamie went to a yoga class near her home twice a week. To reach her class, she had the choice of walking through a park or taking the longer route along the road. She lived in an upscale neighborhood, so she felt safe walking through the park.

As winter approached, the days grew shorter. At Jamie's northerly altitude, it wasn't long before the sun was setting at five o'clock in the evening.

One day as she was walking to her class, Jamie thought she saw a shadowy figure leaning against a tree. She ignored it, knowing it was unusual for someone to be loitering in the park on a cold winter evening. That was her mistake.

The figure stepped forward, flashed a knife and demanded Jamie's purse.

Jamie froze. At first, she didn't register what was happening. A second later, she panicked. She tore her purse off her shoulder, threw it at the mugger and ran away as fast as she could.

Jamie's instinctive reaction was wise. The mugger went for the purse, not her, and Jamie was able to give the police a full account of the mugging.

## When threatened with violence, run away. If you can't run, fight dirty—then run.

There's no way to describe exactly what to do when faced with violence, because every person and every incident of violence is unique. The only advice I can give consistently is to react as the situation warrants. Also, be prepared not to react at all. Many people, especially those not used to dealing with violence, freeze from the psychological shock of being attacked. Consider taking a self-defense course to hone your reflexes and be better prepared. I can describe some pointers, but these are only options, not instructions.

If a situation begins to escalate into violence, there are three things you should try to do:
1) Create distance from your assailant.
2) Gain control of the situation: talk to your assailant, listen to what he has to say, determine what's threatening and what isn't, and find his vulnerabilities.
3) Look for escape routes.

See if you can talk your way out of the situation. Your brain is as much of a weapon as your physical strength. Start from a point of agreement—remember that *everyone* believes he or she is correct—and listen to what the other person has to say. Talking can buy time and help you determine the other person's weaknesses. However, if you're dealing with a stalking situation, don't supply any words that might be seen as encouragement. In this case, it's best to firmly say no or nothing at all.

If talking fails, the best tactic is to forget about heroics and run. Your personal belongings aren't worth getting hurt over. If you're being mugged, throw your purse behind your attacker and run in the opposite direction. Save your dignity for another day.

Attract attention any way you can. If there are people nearby, yell "Fire!" regardless of the crime being committed. It's a sad fact that a cry of "Help!" or "Rape!" will often be ignored. Also, consider carrying a whistle, which can be heard over longer distances and over more noise, than your voice. The Fox-40 whistle, often used at sporting events and usually available in camping stores, is loud and reliable.

Sometimes, witnesses will watch a crime in progress, but do nothing, especially if they're part of a crowd of observers. In this case, American psychologist Robert Cialdini suggests singling people out. Call to "the lady with the stroller" or "the man in the red shirt" to phone the police or come to your aid. By enlisting the help of individuals, it's much harder for them to refuse.

If talking doesn't work, you're unable to escape and you're absolutely forced to defend yourself physically, fight dirty. Target the vulnerable areas of the body: eyes, throat and crotch. Most people have a natural instinct to protect their eyes if you're clawing at them, and this can provide enough of a distraction for you to make an escape. Crotch shots can be painful when you kick hard and have good aim. However, since most attackers are well aware of their vulnerability in this area, don't rely on it as a knockout tactic—especially if you're not sure you can withdraw your foot fast enough to ensure it's not grabbed. Also, look for objects in the vicinity to keep you safe. In a home or restaurant, a chair or barstool can help keep an attacker at a distance, so that he can't grab you. Once you've cleared a path for escape, run.

Since surprise can work to your advantage, don't warn attackers that you'll fight back or that you're trained in self-defense. Don't immediately assume a defensive stance or display threatening gestures unless you need to. If you catch your attacker off-guard, it can buy enough time to escape.

Try this exercise the next time you're walking down the street. Pretend that every third person who walks past you wants to mug you. If they attacked, what would you do? How could you avoid getting close to them in the first place? Where could you escape to and who could you call for help?

Next, reverse roles. If you were a mugger, who would you target? Is it the elderly gentleman with a wooden cane, the mother pushing a stroller or the jogger listening to music on a portable CD player? Where would you hide to make an ambush? How would you make sure your demands were met? What would you do if your victim screamed for help or fought back?

Viewing the world through the eyes of a criminal can be an instructive experience, but remember, it's only an exercise. A criminal views the world through those eyes every minute he's awake.

## Summary

Walk smoothly and confidently to avoid being targeted. Practice awareness. Stay close to populated areas or open businesses, especially at night.

If faced with violence, keep talking and looking for an escape. Keep your assailant at a distance. Attract attention any way you can. If you're attacked, fight dirty. Then run.

# Chapter 4:
# On the Road

Lynda was driving down a suburban road, when a male driver pulled up beside her, rolled down his window and gestured for her to do the same. As she rolled down her window, he pointed to her tires.

"Your tire's flat!" he shouted.

This came as a surprise to Lynda, since she hadn't realized anything was wrong with her car. It looked, sounded and handled normally. She continued driving, with an uneasy feeling, as the other driver kept trying to convince her to pull over. Could she be wrong about the tire?

Although Lynda knew she could damage her car by driving with a flat tire, her intuition told her that the other driver's intentions weren't good. She kept driving until she reached a shopping mall, where she pulled into the parking lot. The other driver didn't follow, but drove past without slowing.

When Lynda stepped out to check, she saw that her tires were perfectly well inflated. She could only guess why the other driver had wanted her to pull over. By sticking to what she knew was true in the face of another person's false statements and by following her intuition when it told her something was wrong, Lynda had kept herself out of harm's way.

What if she'd actually had a flat tire that she hadn't noticed? Her actions still would have taken her to a better place to get help. The parking lot of a busy shopping mall is safer than the shoulder of most roads.

## Know what to do in emergencies

Even the most careful driver can be faced with emergency situations caused by random or unanticipated events. If you're driving alone and find yourself in such a situation, use your common sense.

If your vehicle breaks down, get off the road and out of the path of oncoming traffic, even if you have to drive on a flat tire. A tire is replaceable; you're not. Turn on your emergency flashers and consider using emergency roadway flares if you have them. If you have a cell phone, use it immediately to call for help. If not, use a nearby roadside telephone if one's available. Otherwise, remain in your vehicle with the doors locked and wait for a police officer to stop and help you. If a motorist stops to offer assistance, don't open the window more than a crack, but ask the motorist to call for a tow truck or the police. If you see a stranded motorist, don't stop to help. Carjackers and other criminals sometimes pose as drivers in need of assistance. Call the police to alert them that a motorist is in trouble.

To prevent unexpected breakdowns, check your oil frequently and have your car serviced regularly. Always maintain at least a half tank of gas. Get to know the signs of mechanical problems as they're happening, such as a strange vibration or odor, or a steering wheel that suddenly handles differently. Watch the indicator lights and gauges in your dashboard for any unusual activity. If the problem isn't urgent, drive to a service station rather than stopping on the shoulder of the road. Keep emergency supplies in your vehicle, including a blanket, bottled water and a first aid kit, in case you need to stop unexpectedly.

If your car is bumped from behind or if it's struck in any suspicious way, remain inside with the doors locked, windows rolled up and emergency flashers on. Striking a car from behind can be a ruse to get you out of your car for a carjacking or other crime. Don't get out unless someone in authority arrives or there are many other people—not from the other vehicle—nearby. If you're suspicious and able to drive away, do so, and call the police immediately to report the incident.

## Stay safe when driving

At stop signs and traffic lights, always keep your vehicle in gear so you can accelerate forward at any time. Keep alert. Carjackers often target cars when they're stopped at an intersection. Be ready to drive away—carefully—even if it means running a red light or stop sign. Remember to leave room between yourself and the car in front of you, so you can turn out and make an escape.

Plan and memorize the route you're going to take when traveling and plan an alternative route in case the road's blocked. You don't want to get lost. Remember where police stations and fire stations are and know where to find twenty-four hour gas stations or stores, in case you're out late and need to find a place where there are other people.

Keep your car doors locked and your windows rolled up except for a crack when you want fresh air. Keep your car keys and house keys on separate key chains. If your car's stolen with the keys in the ignition, you don't want your house keys in the hands of the criminal.

If you're suspicious about a situation or think you're being followed, note the other vehicle's license plate number and drive to either a busy, well-lit area or a police station.

Road rage can cause normally law-abiding drivers to perform

dangerous or even violent actions. To avoid causing road rage, be a courteous, alert driver. Don't tailgate and be careful not to cut other drivers off. Drive at the appropriate speed for the lane you're in. If you're driving so slowly that there's a long line of cars behind you, switch to the lane to your right.

Use your horn only to warn of danger, not as a sign of your displeasure after the danger has passed.

In a parking garage outside a shopping mall, a young woman was walking back to her car with her purchases. As she approached her vehicle, a man who looked to be in his sixties called to her from beside a car parked several rows away. He looked like he was in trouble, and he told the young woman that he'd fallen down and needed help getting up.

Sensing that something wasn't right, she told the man that she'd get help. Even as the young woman was walking away, the man continued calling out for her help, saying that he needed her assistance immediately. However, following her instincts, she continued to walk away.

Close to the mall, she found a group of shoppers and told them that an older man needed assistance. As she pointed to where he'd fallen, she saw his vehicle drive quickly away.

The young woman reported the incident to the police, giving a description of the man and his vehicle. A short distance away, a police cruiser stopped the car, finding two middle-aged men and a set of disguises. Upon further investigation, police discovered that the driver had been wearing makeup to make him look older, and that the second man had been hiding behind a nearby vehicle.

It's a commendable trait to want to help other people and it's insidious that criminals exploit this trait to take advantage of people who are helpful. However, it happens. When you're alone, be cautious of anyone who tries to enlist your aid and always trust your gut instinct.

## Protect yourself in parking lots and parking garages

Criminals often lurk in parking lots and parking garages. There are hiding places between cars and often very few people to witness a crime. More important, a parking lot is full of valuable and mobile vehicles worth thousands or tens of thousands of dollars. It's an ideal place for crime to occur.

Always park in areas that are well-lit and visible to other people. Avoid parking next to a van's sliding doors, since these doors make abductions easy. Vans, as well as trucks and other large vehicles, can also block your line of sight. Make sure you have the best visibility possible and that other people can see you as well. Criminals don't want witnesses.

If you must leave your keys with a valet or parking attendant, leave only the ignition key. Don't leave anything in your car with your name, address or other personal identifier on it. An unscrupulous employee can copy your key and later steal your car from your driveway.

Always have your keys in hand, prepared for use, when you're returning to your vehicle. If you have a lot of parcels, groceries or other items with you, get someone you know and trust to walk with you to your vehicle. Consider asking a building security guard or parking lot attendant to escort you to your car, especially when you're alone at night. If no one's available, walk quickly to your vehicle and remain alert.

If you're wearing high heels, change to low flats or running shoes, so you can run if necessary. If someone suspicious approaches you before you can get into your car, yell or scream and run to a place where people can see you. If you can't run away, roll under your car and stay there until help arrives.

As soon as you get into your car, lock your doors and pull away. If anyone's been watching you, this reduces the time they have to attempt a carjacking. Similarly, when you pull into a parking spot, leave your doors locked and engine running until you're ready to exit the car, so you can drive away if you're approached by anyone suspicious.

Look around your vehicle for any irregular activity. Before getting into your car, look around your vicinity, in the back seat and at the passenger side floor. If you see someone loitering near your vehicle, leave the area or walk past your vehicle without stopping and return later. Be suspicious of anyone approaching your vehicle, even if they're doing something seemingly innocuous, such as distributing flyers. If someone calls out to you for assistance in either a parking garage or an outside parking lot, don't approach them. Instead, say that you'll get help and leave immediately to do so. If you see anything suspicious or if something doesn't feel right, leave immediately and contact security or the police.

If you're parked someplace that makes you concerned for your safety, consider calling a friend or relative before returning to you vehicle. Let them know where you are and what you're doing, and call them back once you've left the area safely. However, it's easier and safer in most cases to park near a busy, well-lit area to begin with, rather than taking precautions afterwards.

## Take precautions against car theft

Out of more than a million cars stolen each year in the United States, forty percent have keys in the ignition and eighty percent are left unlocked. Taking the simple precautions of removing the keys from the ignition and locking your vehicle, really do make it more difficult for someone to steal your car.

Hotwiring, as seen in the movies, rarely occurs today. Now, most cars are designed to make hotwiring difficult. Instead of hotwiring a car, thieves usually try to obtain its key, sometimes breaking into a house to do so. Never leave keys openly near the door of your house. Don't keep spare keys hidden in the car or under the hood either, since thieves know about these hiding places.

Make sure the doors are locked and windows closed before leaving your vehicle unattended. Even if you don't have valuables inside, someone might enter your car and hide in ambush.

Consider using a steering wheel lock, such as The Club. The extra hassle of removing such a device can easily convince a car thief to move to another target. Also consider having a car alarm or immobilizer professionally installed. If you're thinking about installing a new car stereo, consider one with a removable faceplate, allowing you to take the faceplate with you whenever you leave the vehicle. Without the faceplate, the stereo is nearly worthless to a thief and you might save yourself the cost of replacing the stereo and a new window.

In general, park in busy, well-lit areas that are highly visible to other people. At home, however, park your car in the garage, since your car is much less likely to be stolen from your garage than from the street. When you park in public, turn your front wheels sharply to the left or right to make it more difficult for thieves to tow your vehicle away.

Always lock your valuables in the trunk or take them with you. Don't leave anything in the body of the car, not even clothing. Thieves recognize that an old jacket thrown across the rear seat might be concealing a laptop computer, so don't take the risk.

Carry your vehicle registration and insurance cards with you, so that if your car's stolen, *you* have proof of ownership—not the thief. Don't leave these documents in the glove box. Copy your Vehicle Identification Number (VIN) somewhere accessible and know your license plate number, in case you ever need to report these to the police.

## Summary

Prepare yourself for emergencies, then if a breakdown occurs, wait for the police to come. Politely decline help from strangers.

Keep your doors locked and windows rolled up at all times. Be especially careful in parking lots and parking garages.

Make it harder to steal your car and don't keep valuables in the body of the car.

# Chapter 5:
# When You're at Home

Young Audri was sleeping over with two of her friends, Melinda and Carol. The family wasn't well off, so the girls stayed in a room on the first floor of the house, with an old door leading to the backyard. The door had a lock, which provided some assurance of security, but it also had a window.

As they were about to go to sleep, one of the girls suddenly exclaimed, "Who's that at the window?"

The others thought she was joking, but when they looked, they saw a man, watching them through the window in the door.

Audri was too petrified to do anything and Melinda was so scared, she jumped into her older sister's bed. Carol was the only one with the presence of mind to scream.

Of course, this brought their mother flying into the room. The man ran away and the girls were ushered into the living room, where the mother called the police.

It was sometime before any of them could get to sleep that night.

It's hard to predict how any of us will react when faced with danger. The three girls displayed three different instinctual reactions. In the end, it was Melinda's scream that brought help. It's rare that a criminal wants to be noticed, so attracting attention to his presence, in any way you can, can be a deterrent.

## Secure your home and belongings

One in ten homes will be broken into this year. In the United States, over thirty percent of all assaults occur during a home invasion and sixty percent of all reported rapes occur during a home invasion. Breaking and entering (B&E) is a crime of opportunity. You can eliminate the opportunity by making your home more difficult to break into.

Visibility is a burglar's enemy. To secure the perimeters around your home, install bright outdoor lights and keep your yard clean. Prune shrubbery, so it doesn't hide windows and doors, allowing thieves to break in without being seen. Cut down tree limbs that a thief could use to access an upper level of your home. Don't leave a ladder outside your house. Consider getting a dog, or at least a *Beware of Dog* sign. The threat of injury is as strong a deterrent as the threat of detection.

A large apartment building can house hundreds of tenants, who frequently change. Try to build a sense of community with your tenant neighbors. If you recognize your neighbors, you'll know who should be in the building and who shouldn't. Don't hold the lobby door open for strangers, but politely ask them to use a key or buzz a resident. Organize citizen patrols to walk around the apartment complex and alert police to suspicious activities. Parking lots, stairways, laundry rooms and playgrounds should receive the most attention. Check for burnt-out lightbulbs, dark corridors and broken locks on mailboxes and doors. Pressure building management to provide adequate security and report all safety issues and breaches of security to management. Participate in a Neighborhood Watch program or start a safe haven program for children to identify places where they can go in an emergency or scary situation.

No matter where you live, keep track of your possessions. If they're stolen, recovery is easier if you can positively identify them. Take pictures of heirlooms and other valuable items you own. Mark or etch all electronic equipment with a unique identification number. If your city's police department has an Operation Identification program for labeling valuable goods, use it. Alternatively, use a unique combination of numbers that are meaningful to you. For example, IBTH102298 could be derived from the phrase, "I Bought This House October 22, 1998." Don't use your Social Insurance/Security Number, since thieves could easily use it to steal your identity and good credit, which are much more valuable than your stereo or DVD player.

If you discover a break-in in progress, don't put yourself at risk by confronting the thief. A criminal who's discovered in the act of committing one crime, might irrationally commit another, such as rape, robbery, assault or even murder. If something looks questionable—a slit screen, a broken window or an open door— don't go in. Call the police from a neighbor's house, your cell phone or a public phone. Don't touch anything or attempt to straighten things up before police arrive, because you might be destroying valuable evidence.

If you think you hear someone breaking into your home, leave safely if you can and then call the police. If you can't leave, lock yourself in a room with a phone and call the police from there. Consider making a loud noise to scare the intruder away. If you wake up at night and see an intruder in your room, it's quite possible he only wants your possessions and doesn't want to commit a more serious crime by hurting you. Judge the situation and if you think he'll leave you alone, pretend to be asleep and call the police after he leaves.

Stephanie was taking her trash out to the dumpsters behind her apartment building, when she noticed a strange man trailing her. Something about him raised her hackles, so she followed her intuition and watched him out of the corner of her eye. Sure enough, when she headed back into the building, he tried to follow her. She stopped and turned around.

"Excuse me," Stephanie said. "Do you have a key?"

"Nah," he said. "I know someone in the building."

"Well then, why don't you go to the front? I'm sure they'll buzz you in."

"But you're going in."

Stephanie was normally a friendly person, but the stranger made her suspicious. She'd lived in bad neighborhoods before, so she knew when she was being set up. She snapped, "Since I live here and I have a *key*, I'm allowed in. That's why I pay rent. I'm sure you can get into the building where *you* pay rent."

"Man, that's not cool of you. C'mon."

*"No. Go to the front and buzz!"*

"Fine, bitch."

He backed off and Stephanie entered the building. As she turned to shut the door behind her, the man tried to grab it from the other side. They had a brief tug-of-war, but Stephanie had a bad grip on the door and couldn't pull it closed. Through the two inches of open door, she shouted, "Let *go* of the door! You're *not* getting in."

The man swore at her again and let go of the door. It closed with a resounding *click*, locking him on the other side.

Stephanie responded to the situation as she thought appropriate and it worked for her. Other women might not have been as blunt, but as long as they realize what's going on and stand their ground, they can convince a would-be invader to move to an easier target.

## Locks keep honest people honest

If you've ever locked yourself out of your home and looked for a way in, then you've seen your home through the eyes of a burglar. Chances are you saw enough ways to get in to feel a little frightened. If you can break in, so can a burglar.

In about fifty percent of all residential burglaries, thieves simply breezed in through unlocked doors or windows. The obvious solution is to use your locks, but those are only effective for that fifty percent of cases. Locks won't deter someone who's intent on circumventing them. Simple door locks can be opened by using a credit card to pry aside the tongue of the lock. If you have any outside doors with this kind of lock, install a deadbolt lock that fits inside the door jamb at least one inch to make the door more secure. Sliding doors are also vulnerable. Place a metal bar or a wooden dowel rod along the door track to prevent the door from being opened or install a pin in the door itself, so it can't be lifted out of its track. Sliding glass doors should have impact-resistant glass for security and safety. Other outside doors should be made of metal or solid wood for strength and equipped with a peephole for observation.

You should be especially aware of doors that aren't visible from the street or from neighbors. Garage doors should be closed and securely locked at all times. The door leading from the garage to the house is a common entry point for burglars and should be kept locked.

One common method of bypassing a lock is by smashing a window, putting a hand through the opening and unlocking the door from the inside. To prevent this, replace windows in your doors and windows beside your doors with impact-resistant glass or plastic. Alternatively, cover them with decorative metal grates with openings too small to put a hand through.

Be careful with your keys. Never hide a spare key in your mailbox, under your doormat or anywhere else outside your home. Thieves know about these hiding places. Instead, give your spare key to a trusted neighbor. If you move into a new house or apartment, or if you lose your house keys, change the locks.

Don't put identification tags on your key chain, except for anonymous tags such as the ones distributed by the War Amps. If the person who finds your keys has criminal intentions and your address is written on your key chain, that person could enter your home. Similarly, when you leave your car for valet parking or repairs, leave only your car's ignition key; don't provide your house keys. An unscrupulous employee can find your address by rifling through the contents of your glove box, make a quick wax imprint of your house keys and enter your home at a later date.

## Staying safe on the telephone

Telephones are convenient, but they can also be a way for criminals to contact you or discover information about you from behind a mask of anonymity. To prevent unwanted telephone calls, get an unlisted number and ask for your name to be removed from reverse directories published by telephone companies and direct marketers. To screen unwanted calls, subscribe to caller ID and call blocking features through your telephone company. You can also use an answering machine to screen calls.

If you're alone and receive a call from an unidentified caller, never indicate that you are alone, because the caller could be planning a crime. Don't give information to "wrong number" callers who ask what number they've dialed.

If you receive an obscene or nuisance call, say nothing and hang up immediately. It could simply be an immature prank, but if the calls persist, refer to the chapter on stalking for methods of dealing with harassing phone calls.

Never verify personal information, like your home address or income, over the telephone, especially if you didn't initiate the call. If you're asked to respond to a survey, ask for the caller's name, the name of the company he represents, and the company's phone number. Then suggest that you call him back.

Be cognizant when you receive a number of telephone calls on your answering machine and no one leaves a message, or if you get a rash of hang-up calls when you're home. While they could be caused by a flawed telemarketing dialing system, they could also indicate that a thief is trying to determine your routine to find the best time to break into your home.

## Summary

Lock your doors and windows, and be protective of your keys. Keep the doors and windows around your home visible and well lit. Befriend your neighbors. Stay alert on the telephone and consider using screening devices if you're being harassed.

# Chapter 6:
# On the Job

After Donna graduated from a state university with a degree in sociology, she didn't see many options for immediate employment. So when a friend told her about a temp agency that was hiring people with little experience, she filled out an application. Three weeks later, she accepted a placement as an administrative assistant at a small advertising agency. It wasn't her dream job, but since she was still learning about the world, she reasoned that any work experience was valuable.

Between filing and photocopying, Donna kept herself busy by learning as much about the advertising industry as she could. She took an interest in projects, listened to conversations and flipped through the industry journals she found around the office. Her boss noticed her interest and gave her assignments of increasing responsibility.

One of the younger account executives also took notice. Whenever he saw Donna working on a project, he casually asked how much longer she'd be working at their agency.

"We'll miss you when you have to leave," he said.

Donna smiled and tried not to let his comments bother her, but it didn't always work. Who was she to have ambitions at this agency? She was only a temp and she could be assigned to a different job at any time. She found it harder to focus on her work with these thoughts filling her mind.

The account executive seemed to take glee in Donna's flagging work performance. As her efforts declined, he made increasingly derisive comments about her eventual firing from the company. Donna became irritable, stressed and exhausted.

Finally, Donna's boss called her into his office, concerned about her performance. Donna admitted that she had a problem and then sheepishly described her experiences with the account executive.

Her boss was livid. This account executive had caused problems previously. Earlier in the year, the young man had threatened another employee and as a condition of his continued employment, he'd been told to mend his ways. Donna was cleared of all misdoings and the account executive was fired.

## Become aware of the different forms of harassment and violence

When we think of workplace violence, we often think of the psychotic employee who snaps under the stress of his job and guns down half a dozen of his co-workers. Although such violence is sensationalized in the media, it's rare. Workplace violence is often psychological. Bullying, threats and harassment are all forms of psychological violence. Harassment is any behavior that irritates, embarrasses, intimidates or degrades. Women are often targets of sexual harassment, but harassment can also be based on race, religion, sexual orientation or disability.

Sexual harassment falls under two categories: hostile work environment and *quid pro quo*. A hostile work environment is one in which inappropriate sexual suggestions, such as pornographic images, vulgar language, dirty jokes or unwelcome touching, make an employee feel uncomfortable. *Quid pro quo,* Latin meaning "something for something," refers to a sexual demand in exchange for employment benefits or even employment itself. Laws in the US and Canada protect employees from both forms of sexual harassment.

Physical violence, although less common than harassment, can usually be predicted. Watch for fellow employees who are jealous of you or your accomplishments, who have an unusual interest in weapons, who abuse drugs or alcohol, who seem socially inept or constantly negative, whose work performance is declining or whose behavior or attitudes have changed drastically. Be especially aware of any kind of threats or intimidation, since these often precede violence. These early warning signs are only guidelines, however. An employee might show all these signs and never harm anyone; conversely, he might erupt into violence without showing any of them.

Larger companies usually have a policy for dealing with workplace violence and harassment. If there isn't a policy in place, recommend that one be drafted. Make sure it includes specific definitions of harassment and violence, the responsibilities of management and employees to ensure a safe and comfortable workplace, procedures for registering a complaint, a guarantee of protection from punishment for anyone who makes a complaint and the steps to take in case of an emergency.

Evaluate physical security at your workplace. Make changes, if you're in a position to do so, or suggest them to someone who is. For instance, consider installing closed-circuit cameras, bright lights in the parking lot or silent panic buttons to summon help. Security guards posted at the entrance, reception or customer service areas can deter violence or step in quickly if it happens. In lieu of a silent alarm, you can agree with your co-workers to a code word that serves as a distress signal. Your co-worker can then summon police or security while you buy time.

## Deal immediately with workplace violence and harassment

Report violence or harassment to someone in the company who's in a position of authority, normally your supervisor. Check your company's policy. If your immediate supervisor doesn't handle your complaint to your satisfaction, go to that person's manager. If there's a union, go to the union steward; if not, contact your local Human Rights Commission or Commission on Civil Rights. Know your rights as an employee.

If you're continually being threatened, bullied or harassed, record every incident in a journal. Include dates, times and possible witnesses. Collect evidence, such as damaged property, if it's available. This can help prove your case.

Get emotional support from friends, family and anyone else who will listen. Crisis centers and sexual assault centers can offer help to women who are harassed in the workplace. Seeking help or support from trusted co-workers is appropriate, but be careful confiding in anyone who has a conflict of interest.

## Reprise: Everyone thinks he or she is right

If you find yourself in a verbal conflict with a co-worker or customer, listen carefully to what the other person has to say and respond appropriately. Ask sincere, open-ended questions to find out what they're complaining about. Give her your full attention. Don't blindly repeat one line, such as "It's company policy," like a mantra. Has this approach ever satisfied you when you were on the receiving end?

A better approach is to ask the other person what you could do to solve the problem, handle the complaint or ease her mind. If the request is reasonable, the solution is obvious. Allowing the other person to be part of the solution makes them feel empowered and helps defuse the tension of the situation.

When you're gathering information, avoid asking *why* questions, which look toward the past, invite rationalizations and are sometimes confrontational: "Why did you take so long to complete the task?" Instead, ask *how* a situation can be improved. A more useful question would be, "How can we make better use of your time?" *How* questions lead to future solutions.

Think in terms of "Yes, and…" rather than "Yes, but…" In general, try to avoid the word "but." It has a tendency to negate everything previously stated: "You're a model employee and your performance is superb, but your shoes don't match your belt."

Think win-win. In many cases, it's possible to fulfill both your goals and the other person's. Find a higher purpose or an ultimate goal that you share with the other person and work from there to find a mutually satisfactory solution. Focus on outcomes, rather than the people involved or what happened in the past, since those can't be changed anyway.

If you've exhausted all your other options, consider passing the customer's case to a supervisor. This action alone indicates that you're doing something to address the customer's concerns, and may ease her mind.

Consider this scenario: As your husband's mowing the lawn with the new lawnmower you bought for his birthday, its blade comes loose and flies across the yard, narrowly missing your arm and shattering a window. You're fuming mad when you call the manufacturer to complain. You want to see heads roll—yours almost did! Calmly and professionally, the customer service representative says, "We'll look into the matter and ensure that it doesn't happen again." Are you satisfied?

What if the representative apologetically says, "I'm so sorry it happened. I'll see to it that it doesn't happen again"?

Now, how would you feel if the representative *angrily* said, "That's outrageous! You have every right to be upset! I *will* make sure it never happens again!"

In most cases, the *angry* sounding representative will win the customer's trust and calm her down. This is very different from losing your temper or getting into an argument with a customer. This shows agreement and understanding on an emotional level.

## Use tact with angry customers

If an angry customer confronts you, remember that no matter how unreasonable she seems, she believes she's right and will act as if that's the most obvious thing in the world. To understand her concerns, you have to adopt the "customer's always right" mindset. Gain rapport with the other person by subtly matching her tone of voice and body language, even if it means slightly raising your voice. You're not trying to get into an argument, since your words will be agreeable, but you're demonstrating that you recognize her concerns.

*After* you gain rapport with the customer, soften your voice to calm her down. If you begin the confrontation by speaking in a calm voice, the customer isn't likely to feel she's understood. She might become more aggressive to make her point.

Virginia Satir, a family therapist, identified five main modes of communication. A person's dominant mode varies in different situations, but stressful arguments tend to bring out the worst in people. These modes have self-explanatory names: 1) Blamer, 2) Distracter, 3) Placater, 4) Computer and 5) Leveler. An angry customer is likely a Blamer or a Distracter. A Placating, or passive and yielding, strategy might seem like a good way of dealing with this customer, but in some cases, this only gives the other person an increased sense of righteousness.

If you're ever unsure how to respond in a high-tension situation, linguist Suzette Haden Elgin suggests that the Computer mode of vague, impersonal and neutral language ("Certainly, one can see that such a matter is often problematic.") is the safest strategy. If the customer baits you with personal remarks, ignore them. Speaking this way drains all the emotion from any argument.

## Summary

Become aware of the different forms of violence and harassment. Read your company's policy on workplace violence, if it has one, or suggest drafting a policy if not. Watch for the early signs that a co-worker or regular customer might become violent.

Report incidents of harassment or violence and keep records to help support your complaint. Enlist support from people you trust.

In a verbal conflict, listen carefully, think win-win and gain rapport with the other person. Failing that, go into Computer mode.

# Chapter 7:
# Around the World

Whenever I travel, I enjoy the sport of "people watching." Maybe you do too. We can learn many things from observing others: their culture, their attitudes, and how they react differently from us to situations. This applies as much to people in your homtown as it does to people abroad, but watching people from a different culture has an added appeal.

You can also learn about safety from others, simply by observing them. In this chapter, I'll discuss how to blend in when you're away from home by watching and emulating how the locals behave. It's not always the locals you should be watching, however. Try picking out and observing the habits of other visitors. They're easy to pinpoint, especially North Americans. If you have time to spare, follow them around—on the street, in and out of stores, and near tourist areas—pretending you're a criminal, and calculate how easy it would be for you to rob one of them. Learn from their mistakes.

A while ago, I was traveling in Rome, my favorite city and one of the most dangerous for travelers. At about one o'clock in the afternoon, I noticed a group of four women casually walking down the Via Della Maddalena, towards the Pantheon and Piazza Della Rotunda. They were obviously tourists. Their mannerisms, speech, body language and cameras were a dead giveaway. I followed them for a short distance for two reasons: one, to see how long it would take for something to happen and two, to render assistance if necessary.

As they were approaching the piazza from the north side,

an old woman appeared directly in front of them, seemingly out of nowhere. She asked for handouts politely, but when the tourists tried to bypass her, she began to yell and swear. The tourists, obviously unprepared for this, were momentarily disoriented. That's when a second group of young women joined the fray. I guess you could say it was a swarming, Italian style.

Within seconds, it was over. Cameras were stolen, a handbag or two were taken and four very frightened young women were left standing at the edge of the piazza. The young culprits dispersed in different directions and the old woman, who was likely a young girl in disguise, had disappeared without a trace. I was amazed at how quickly it happened.

Although there's sometimes safety in numbers, you still have to take appropriate precautions. Know your surroundings and plan for potential problems or it's very easy to fall victim to predators.

## Know the cons

No matter where you travel, including in the airports, bus stations and train stations, watch out for this kind of technique. South American pickpocket gangs travel Europe all summer and North America in the fall and early winter, using all sorts of ruses to distract travelers and steal their wallets and purses.

Be alert to the person who walks up to you and asks for the time or the person who inadvertently spills ice cream or condiments (a.k.a., The Ketchup Gang) on your blouse or sweater. When you look down, it gives an accomplice the opportunity to rush in and pick your pocket. Also, be wary of the single mother who appears to be having trouble with a baby.

When you offer assistance and need to put your bags down, they're stolen.

I was involved in the arrest of one of these gangs not long ago. It was about a week before Christmas, a busy time for travelers. Information led us to a safe house in the city, where we'd been told there was a stash of property taken from people victimized at the airport.

What we found was amazing. In less than two weeks of operation, this gang of thieves from Chile had stolen credit cards, passports, cameras, video equipment, bottles of liquor, clothing, more than $25,000 in cash and literally anything someone might carry with them on vacation. Fortunately for us, they hadn't arranged to sell the property prior to our visit, or all of it would have been converted to cash.

Although there've been numerous alerts dispatched by various police and other law enforcement agencies alerting people to this type of crime, it's still as rampant today as it was ten years ago.

## Think and act like a local

Some of the most memorable travel experiences stem from taking chances, trusting strangers and opening yourself up to the world. However, you have to take into account the social and religious customs of the countries you visit. Otherwise, they may affect your safety or even your freedom.

As soon as you step off familiar turf, you may find yourself guided by a new set of gender rules. For example, in some countries it may be socially unacceptable for a woman to be outside alone at night. In other countries, it may be unheard of for a woman to travel alone. What's more, many cultures view Western women as loose, promiscuous and easy sexual prey.

When you're exploring other cultures, whether for business or pleasure, adapt to local customs to avoid these kinds of perceptions. Sometimes, this requires a change in how you dress, where you go, and how and with whom you speak.

No matter where you go, keep a low profile and look like you belong there. Thieves and scam artists circle around tourists like vultures. Don't attract attention to yourself with your clothing. Avoid wearing a combination of leisure and business attire, such as jeans and business shoes, because this can make you look like a displaced business traveler. Dress down and dress to blend in. Observe local women and make note of how they dress. For instance, don't bare your arms and legs if local women don't. It's not necessary to go out in native dress, except in several Middle Eastern countries, but don't flaunt Western fashions or habits. Avoid wearing jewelry, especially necklaces, which can be used to hold you by the neck. However, a simple, unadorned wedding ring can ward off unwanted advances; consider buying a cheap, gold-plated band for this purpose. Never go into a marginal neighborhood wearing anything that stands out. Even if you're of a different ethnic background, it's better to give the impression that you live and work there than to look like someone who's just visiting.

Even when you're on unfamiliar territory, act as if you know exactly where you are and where you're going. Appearing lost or confused may make you an easy target. As always, walk with purpose. Don't wander around like you're sightseeing. Study a map before you go out and ask the hotel concierge or a female employee to mark any dangerous areas to avoid. If you have to study a map on the street, discreetly use a mini-sized pocket guide to avoid looking like a tourist. Always be aware of your surroundings and the people around you and consider traveling in a group of two or more for greater safety.

Also be conscious of what your nonverbal signals might represent—you don't want to attract unwanted attention. A friendly gesture or a casual touch that's perfectly acceptable in your hometown, might be viewed as a sexual advance by someone in a different culture. In some cultures, simply making eye contact with a man is a signal that you want his company; sunglasses can help you avoid making this mistake.

Pre-plan your trip. Prepare yourself by learning what to expect and what aspects of the local culture might be different from what you're accustomed to. Become familiar with your destination's local customs and learn to follow the protocols expected of you. Learn the language. Even a few words in the local language can open doors for you. Memorize courtesies such as "please," "thank you" and "excuse me," as well as phrases important to your safety, such as "I need a doctor," "leave me alone," "help" and "police."

Before you leave, let someone you trust know your itinerary. If you must travel to a country that's in turmoil, off the beaten path, or restricted to visitors, register with the nearest Canadian or American embassy upon arrival. Avoid booking flights that disembark at an unfamiliar airport at night. Many airports are located outside the city and you may have difficulty finding safe, reliable transportation.

## Stay Alert and Intrepid when everything else is new and different

Taking a trip can be a pleasant way of temporarily forgetting your troubles back home, but there's one thing you should never forget: be Alert and Intrepid. When you're walking around a city, keep to busy, well-lit streets and walk facing traffic. If you sense someone's following you, or you're uncomfortable with people in the area, try to find other people and look for the easiest escape.

Be wary of people offering unsolicited help. If you're approached by someone claiming to be a police officer, politely insist to speak to a uniformed officer, even if the person shows you a badge. There've been several cases in which criminals have impersonated police. *Never* follow someone in a different direction from your intended destination.

Don't use a public washroom in an isolated area of a park, subway or train station. Go to a nearby restaurant, like a McDonald's. Consider using the corner stall, so you have fewer sides to defend if you're attacked. Don't hang purses or travel bags on the hooks of toilet stall doors where someone could reach in and grab them.

Keep your luggage close to you and away from the grasp of others. On a train with a sleeping car, keep your valuables with you and try to sleep with an arm or leg resting on your luggage. Be careful around bus stations, train stations, docks and other transportation hubs, since pickpockets target these areas. Any time a stranger bumps into you, unexpectedly engages you in conversation or otherwise distracts you, take a quick *mental* inventory of your valuables. Don't pat your pocket, since this informs criminals where your wallet is.

Carry the minimum number of valuables needed for your trip and carry necessary items such as money, airplane tickets and your passport in a body belt under your clothing. Become familiar with your destination's currency before you have to use it. Change money only at banks and official currency exchangers, not taxis or street stands. Have cash tips ready for porters and doormen so you don't have to pull out your wallet. Divide your money into small denominations and large denominations for smaller and larger purchases. Don't expose large amounts of money in public places; instead, organize your money in the privacy of your room. In foreign countries, try to pay for small purchases with cash or traveler's checks. The less you use your credit cards, the less you need to worry about your credit being used without your knowledge. If you do use your credit card and sign a three-part form, ask the shopkeeper for the carbon copy with your receipt, so that the duplicate doesn't fall into the wrong hands.

If you don't know where you are, try to find a major street or thoroughfare. Police stations, fire stations and hospitals can help you find your way. If you must ask for directions from a stranger, choose a woman, and if you're concerned about being followed, mention that you're meeting your husband or boyfriend at your destination.

If you rent a car, insist on an unmarked vehicle, to avoid advertising to local criminals that you're a tourist. Otherwise, opportunists may follow you or ambush you at a gas station to rob you or steal the car. Always plan your route ahead of time. If you become lost while driving and end up in an area that makes you uncomfortable, do *not* stop, look at a map or ask directions until you reach a busy, well-lit area. To prevent unplanned stops, keep enough gasoline in your tank at all times, especially in rural areas where gas stations may be rare and far apart.

If you return to your car and find the area where you parked is now deserted, if possible, ask someone to escort you to your vehicle. If you must approach the car alone, scan the immediate area and glance into and under the car before getting in. Have your car keys ready, held tightly in your fist, with the tip sticking out and ready to use as a weapon if necessary.

## Watch your drinks

A friend of mine, Melinda, tells a fascinating travel story and has advice for travelers based on her experience:

"When I started traveling, some of my fellow travelers chuckled at my religious attendance to my drinks, especially if I was with a group of travel friends. I rebuked them by responding that it was a habit that could some time prove valuable.

"After two full months of traveling, I ended up in Barcelona after a spectacular car trip through southern France with my brother. After he left, I found myself on my own again and settled into a hostel downtown for company. For the first three nights, fellow travelers accompanied me on both day and night adventures. And these were intoxicating—hundreds of street performers, tapis bars and non-stop wining, dining and dancing until the wee hours of the morning. Many cities don't wake up until after eleven p.m. It's quite normal to want a taste of these nighttime experiences while traveling.

"I was keen to continue seeing and experiencing the thriving Spanish culture, although I hadn't yet met a new travel mate to explore it with. So I bought a ticket to a Flamenco show and went alone. It was a cacophony of the most delightful modern Flamenco I'd ever seen. The show finished at eleven p.m. and I was giddy from the experience.

"As I headed back down the throbbing Las Ramblas, I spotted a bar two doors from my hostel and thought, *Why should being on my own stop me from going in? Perhaps I'll meet an interesting traveler.* The bar was a stone's throw from my hostel, so I was close to my accommodation. Although it was something I seldom did when traveling, I decided to have a nightcap alone with one rule: no more than two glasses of Rioja, even if I met someone and decided to stay.

"Within a couple of minutes of sliding onto a bar stool, two Frenchman had joined me. They were engaging and well dressed. I chatted at length with the one on my left, Joseph. In hindsight, it seemed strange that they sat on either side of me, but you often attribute such things to cultural differences.

"Joseph was a management consultant. He lived in Paris and was fluent in English, Spanish and French. His less social friend, Jean, listened in on my right. We chatted about my recent visit to France and where I came from. He helped me with a few phrases in French. They told me many things about Barcelona, because they'd visited before and we even talked about Flamenco. All this was common chatter for travelers who meet on the road. I was delighted to end my day this way. My initial awkwardness at arriving alone had dissipated and by now, the bar was jam-packed.

"I'd been there almost an hour when I noticed that my glass was still full, even though I'd taken a number of sips. I turned to see Joseph topping it up from a carafe while my back was turned. Smiling, I put my hand over the glass and asked him to stop, saying the glass was my last one and that I'd be leaving soon. I'd had only two short glasses of Rioja and felt quite alert. After that, I became more aware of my glass, keeping an eye on the amount of alcohol in it after every sip.

"The travel chatter faded and they began asking if they could now take me to dinner. I declined, saying I'd eaten earlier. Jean asked me several times and I declined each time. 'Really, I'm not interested,' I said. 'I'll be going soon.' Another of my rules was never to leave a place with a stranger. I really didn't know these guys at all. I wanted to remain close to my accommodation.

"Soon, I began to feel a bit nauseous and woozy, so I asked for my bill and excused myself to go to the washroom. Looking in the mirror, I decided I probably had travel fatigue from many hours of walking and perhaps I was dehydrated too. I wasn't feeling drunk.

"When I returned, Joseph was talking with a woman on his left and Jean swooped in with broken-English tales of his love life… something about the threesomes they'd had with a hotel clerk and equally unsavory feats. The topic and tone had drastically changed. I had a sinking feeling. What a shame. I decided that all good things must come to an end and again, I called for my tab from the bartender. Joseph spoke to him in rapid Spanish and, for the second time, my bill failed to appear. By now, Jean was insisting that I go outside with him. As I refused again, I was startled that my words barely hooked together. My head began a full spin. The music warped in my head and I could barely hear him.

"I looked for my glass. Again, it was full. But now it was near Jean. I'd kept it on my left all night. Like a thunderbolt, I realized that I'd left it unattended to go to the washroom. I couldn't believe my stupidity. By now, my head was heavy and the room seemed to be emitting a blue fog that rolled onto the bar. I felt panicky, my heart pounding. Somehow, I assured myself this was *not* happening to me.

"Jean had stopped asking me to leave with him. He was simply putting on his jacket, pulling me off the stool and telling me that we were going for dinner now. Joseph smirked at him over my head, waved and said, 'I'll join you later.'

"That was it. I knew I was sinking fast and needed to move even faster to get away from them. Through my confusion, of that much I was certain. This is where you forget to mind your manners. By the time Jean turned around with his coat on, I'd disappeared out the front door and was back at my hostel. I didn't even utter a goodbye. And yes, I ran.

"The next morning, I slept through the enchanting bells that echo through the maze of streets near Las Ramblas. Normally, their clatter wakes me instantly. I finally got up at eleven a.m. with a terrible headache and no memory of running the twenty meters to my hostel. No memory of opening the door with my key, saying '*hola*' to the desk clerk or seeing who was back in the six-bed dorm. Nothing. So fuzzy was my thinking, that it wasn't until hours later I realized I'd been drugged and that I'd been damn lucky. Without insisting on keeping my rule about never leaving a place with strangers, I might've woken up somewhere far worse. The consequences could have been very ugly.

"Did it ruin my travels? No. Did it taint the experience? Not a chance. Was I afraid afterwards? Not at all. Did I feel lucky? You bet. Did I ever do that again? Of course. But only close to my accommodation and I watched my drinks like a hawk. I never left a drink unattended again and if I did, I wouldn't touch it when I returned. Those were some of the rules I lived by on the road. And they do work."


Since this experience, Melinda's advice to women travelers is always to watch your drinks. This is especially important for the solo female traveler, and sometimes it's easily forgotten. There's no better way to bond with fellow travelers and meet the locals than going to local watering holes for memories you'll never forget—like downing a pint in Belfast at a local pub with a cage around the door to keep hand-thrown bombs from rolling in. But beware: whether you're sipping tea, wine or beer, watch your drinks at all times.

In fact, if you aren't used to watching your drink, and intend to travel, practice this skill at home before leaving. Make it a rule. Keep your drink in view at all times and know how much is in it. If you leave a crowded place to go to the washroom, and don't have a trusted companion to watch your drink for you, get a new drink when you return. Also, make sure you see the drink poured. Don't accept a drink that mysteriously appears in a glass. Watch it go into the glass. It's an important habit to develop.

When you travel alone, decide on your own rules and stick to them, even if they don't always seem to make sense. Listen actively to what people are saying to you and pay attention to your state of mind at all times, especially if you're on your own without a trusted travel mate. These are the ingredients of savvy travel intuition. You must trust it at all times and not allow these experiences to transcend the exquisite, freeing experience of traveling alone. Your good experiences will far outweigh the bad, if you stick to your rules and pay close attention to your intuition.

When the tone of a conversation makes you uncomfortable, leave. People will let you know their intentions, whether consciously or not, if you're listening carefully. If you feel uncomfortable, forget your manners. Say no often and loudly in as many languages as you travel in.

And if all else fails, walk away, safely and quickly.

## Stay safe in hotels

Look for smaller, more intimate hotels. You want the staff to be familiar with who its guests are and who doesn't belong.

Try to get a sense of how female-friendly the hotel is ahead of time. The hotel should have enough staff to walk you to your room late at night and it should have an attendant in the hotel gym. Reception and concierge desks near the entrance or elevators can deter unwanted visitors.

Look for a parking lot that's well-lit and secure. Alternatively, if there's valet parking, use it so you don't have to walk across a parking lot late at night. It may give you extra peace of mind to choose a hotel that locks its doors at night or has security cameras in the lobby and hallways.

Ask to see your hotel room before taking it and examine it carefully. Does the door lock securely? Does the room feel safe? Do you see any peepholes other than the one in the door? Trust your instincts. Make sure your hotel room door has a peephole and double locks: a regular lock and a dead bolt. Even then, it's a good idea to have a doorstop with you. Request a room that's away from emergency exits, catwalks, terraces, renovation work and any other structures that might make it easier for someone to break in through your window. A room between the second and sixth floors is safest. The first floor might be too easy to break into and fire hoses may not reach above the sixth floor. Look for a safe to store your valuables.

The reception area should afford privacy for guests checking in. You can protect your privacy by registering with your last name and only your first initial. No one should be able to overhear your name, room number or other personal information as you're checking in. Room numbers should be written on the key envelope, not mentioned aloud or inscribed on the key or smart card. If you're worried that others in the lobby have overheard the check-in clerk calling you by name, revealing your room number or giving directions to your room, go to your room and call the front desk to rectify the situation. Explain your concerns, ask for a different room and insist that the key be brought to you. If you take the step of asking the hotel to block your calls, the front desk staff won't reveal your room number to anyone calling in. Guard your key and room number well.

To mark your luggage, use covered tags with your office address, *not* your home address. Frequent travelers may prefer to use specially encoded nameless luggage tags, available by subscription through services similar to the War Amps key program. Don't leave your baggage in the lobby for the porter to bring to your room later, unless your suitcases are locked and your identification tags don't reveal any personal information. If you need to leave your luggage for the porter, even if it's locked, open the bags as soon as they're back in your possession and check for missing items or signs of tampering.

In some European countries, the hotel will ask you to leave your passport at the front desk. In many cases, refusal isn't an option. Ask if the hotel will accept a photocopy of the front page and if so, give them only the copy. If you're forced to leave your original passport, make certain to keep a copy of the front page with you. If there are any loose documents inside the passport, such as visas, ask to keep them or make a copy.

When riding in hotel elevators, stand near the elevator buttons with your back to the side wall. If threatened, push all the buttons at once. The alarm will sound and the elevator door will open at the next floor.

Display the Do Not Disturb sign, even if you aren't in your room, so it looks occupied. *Never* display the Make Up Room sign to announce your absence. Instead, call housekeeping.

If there's a fire in your hotel, avoid using the elevators. Smoke often disables the photocell light beams and makes the doors inoperable. If smoke or flames force you to stay in your room, turn on the bathroom exhaust fan to help clear the smoke and turn off the air conditioner so smoke isn't drawn in from other locations. Fill the bathtub with water, because you might need it if the pipes stop working. Put a wet towel under the door to stop smoke from entering your room. If there are windows fitted one on top of the other, open the bottom window and the top window just a crack. This allows fresh air to come in through the lower window, while smoke can escape from the top.

## Defend the home front

Before you leave home for a vacation or business trip, remember to safeguard your house. You want to keep up the appearance of your daily routine to make thieves believe that you're still at home. Use timers to turn on and off both interior and exterior lights at different times. Leave shades, blinds and curtains in their normal positions. In the summer, arrange to have your lawn mowed periodically; in the fall, have your leaves raked; and in the winter, arrange for your driveway and sidewalk to be shoveled after every snowfall. Either ask the post office to hold your mail or have a neighbor pick it up. Suspend your newspaper delivery and don't leave notices announcing your absence.

## Summary

Learn about the culture you're traveling to and try to blend in by dressing and acting the way local women do. Keep alert anywhere you go. Carry only the valuables you need and keep your money, tickets and passport in a belt underneath your clothing.

No matter where you are in the world, never turn your back on your drink.

Select your hotel carefully and guard your room number well.

Before leaving, make sure your home maintains its lived-in look by setting up timers and asking friends to carry out routine tasks.

# Chapter 8:
# Stalking

Anyone can be a victim of stalking. We usually think of women or celebrities as targets, but men are often victims too. While researching this book, I spoke with several human resources directors and was amazed to find that the proportion of stalking and harassment victims at their companies was split almost evenly between men and women.

Several years ago, I was a victim of stalking. What started as an innocent attempt to help one of my adult students turned into several years of dealing with unwanted phone calls, letters, cards, gifts and finally, her finding my address and watching my house. No, she didn't break in and harm my pets. Still, it was a shock to discover she'd been watching me, since I was a seasoned police veteran and should have known better.

Many men joke that they'd enjoy being stalked by a woman. However, I wasn't looking for an ego boost. I was simply trying to help someone whom I thought needed encouragement and a little assistance to get ahead. There was no physical attraction on my part to complicate matters.

Even though I knew she was going too far, I was afraid to hurt her feelings by giving her a definite no. In my mind, I thought she'd go away on her own. On several occasions when I tried to put a stop to her harassment, she always found a way of making me feel bad. In this respect, I was a classic victim. She played upon my sense of decency; that was my Achilles heel and it made me easy to manipulate.

So what, specifically, did I do wrong? I didn't listen to or act on my intuition. I was afraid to say enough is enough by giving her a definite no. I responded to phone calls, e-mails and requests for meetings. I tried to reason with her, which only gave her an added impetus to escalate when she thought I might be ending our "relationship." I wasn't always aware of my surroundings, especially in my home environment. Worse, I hid my problem from my loved ones. For everyone's security, it would have been better if I had told my friends and family what was happening.

You're probably wondering how it ended. Well, first I took the positive step of telling my wife. Not surprisingly, she was concerned yet totally understanding and it was a relief to have her support. One day, my wife answered my cell phone and my female stalker was on the line. I'll leave the rest to your imagination.

As you read further in this chapter, you'll find suggestions on how to protect yourself from stalking and harassment. If you're presently involved in a stalking situation, I urge you to take appropriate steps immediately. It's important for your peace of mind, your safety and your family's safety.

## Recognize the early warning signs

Look for signs that someone's budding admiration might escalate into serious harassment. My case began innocently enough, with my student constantly asking if she could talk to me after class. Still, I should have seen this as a pattern that might escalate. Soon I was receiving constant phone calls, small gifts and never-ending attention. Since stalkers are literally obsessed with their targets, constant attentiveness is a major warning sign.

There are other warning signs that someone might be inclined to stalk you. Maybe they're too "nice," in the sense that they're emotionally manipulative or place guilt or obligation on you. Similarly, any kind of intense jealousy or anger, for reasons that seem trivial to you, can be a red flag. Furthermore, someone who's too persistent or who can't take no for an answer, is more likely to start stalking you once his other options have been exhausted.

Stalkers prey on vulnerabilities, like an overly empathic personality or an inability to say no. While we've all been taught to be polite, it's sometimes necessary to assert yourself more strongly when you're dealing with someone who doesn't observe the rules of etiquette. Listen to your intuition, especially in the early stages of getting to know someone. If that person makes you feel uncomfortable, ask yourself why.

Rebecca Gilman's recent play, *Boy Gets Girl*, portrays one woman's ordeal with being stalked. In the first act, a magazine reporter named Theresa meets a blind date, Tony, for a beer. Their conversation is awkward, Tony is a little over enthusiastic about winning Theresa's affection, and the result is amusing to watch. By their second meeting, however, it's obvious that Tony is emotionally needy. Sensing their incompatibility, Theresa tells him that she isn't looking for a relationship.

Tony sends flowers to Theresa's office. Soon, he's leaving increasingly desperate, and increasingly threatening, messages on her voice mail. Although Theresa denies she has a problem, a menacing telephone call from Tony finally scares her into calling the police. Initially, the police detective assigned to the case says that she can't help, because Tony hasn't actually done anything illegal, but when his threats escalate, she helps Theresa obtain a restraining order.

Unfortunately, the restraining order isn't effective for long. Tony continues to intrude on Theresa's life, until she's too afraid to even sleep in her own home. Her change from a bubbly, self-confident reporter to a frightened, bewildered woman is astounding.

*Boy Gets Girl* takes its title from the stereotypical Hollywood plotline: boy meets girl, boy loses girl, boy gets girl. Perhaps it's old-fashioned in its sexism, but the ideal of a persistent male suitor appeals to many people of both genders. Some men emulate this pattern in real life, and some of them will be perceived as romantic. But what's the dividing line between romance and stalking? In the play, it's obvious: Tony starts sending Theresa threats. In real life, it's often unclear, unless it reaches this level. Again, if anyone ever makes you uncomfortable, examine the reasons why.

As senseless and unfair as it seems, Theresa has to make drastic changes in her life to deal with the threat of her stalker. Eventually, she has to change her name and move to another city. However, there's one positive aspect to this story; she's never physically harmed, because she takes good precautions and seeks help from others.

## Be firm when dealing with a potential stalker; better yet, ignore him or her

Playing hard to get is common in the game of courtship, so coyness can be read as a sign of encouragement, often accurately. When you're dealing with someone who's uncomfortably persistent, you don't want to confuse him by sending mixed messages. Instead, firmly and consistently say no.

Remember that *everyone* believes he or she is right. No stalker thinks of himself as a stalker and no mirror you can put up to his behavior is likely to show him how deluded he is. Don't insult or try to humiliate him.

If consistently saying no doesn't work, ignore him. Don't try to reason with your stalker, because most likely, he can't be reasoned with. Besides, you don't want any of your communication taken as a sign of encouragement. If harassment's a power game for the stalker, as it often is, any communication on your part is a score for the stalker. Once you decide to cease contact with him, commit to that decision.

## Enlist help from the police

Anti-stalking legislation exists in every jurisdiction in Canada and the United States. If you're being stalked, threatened or harassed, contact the police immediately and provide a detailed report. Consider taking a friend or loved one along for support. If the officer you initially encounter won't take a report, ask to speak with a higher-ranking officer until your complaint is handled to your satisfaction. Take note of who you've spoken with and what was said. If the police make a formal report, ask for a copy.

Threats of violence should be taken seriously. The more detailed the threat is—if it mentions a time, location or method—the more likely it is to be carried out. In Canada, you don't need to prove that your stalker intended to scare you, only that you were scared. However, you do need to prove that your fear is reasonable.

Law enforcement agencies are continually trying to improve how they manage cases involving stalking victims. Leading police forces use threat assessment programs to identify potential perpetrators and assess the risks involved by a given perpetrator at a given time. Their goal is to manage both the stalker and the risks that he or she presents, or might present, to a given target. Let the police advise a course of action based on their knowledge and experience. For instance, seeking a restraining order, while often effective, can anger some stalkers and escalate the situation.

Still, recognize that the police have limited resources. Take your own precautions and watch out for yourself. Even if you get a restraining order, a piece of paper won't stop someone who's gone beyond the threshold of reason.

Keep a record of every activity that threatens or intimidates you, as this can help prove your case in court. Record the date, time, location and any actions or statements made. Include phone calls, e-mails, letters, gifts and any personal encounters. Don't accept gifts if you're given the choice; otherwise, keep them as evidence. When recording phone calls, take notes on the caller's voice and anything else you can hear in the background, like a television program or traffic noise. If possible, videotape the activity or take photos as evidence to corroborate your written log. If any of your property is destroyed or vandalized, take photographs and note the event in your journal.

## Take precautions

One aspect of stalking that makes it different from many other forms of crime discussed in this book is that the perpetrator targets you specifically. This means that many methods of prevention don't work. You can't convince a stalker to find an easier target, the way you might with a burglar. Throughout this book, you've been receiving advice on how to become more aware of crime and how to secure your car and home. It's even more important to take precautions to ensure that you and your family aren't harmed when you're specifically targeted for crime. If you don't know the identity of your stalker, be alert for anyone, whether you know them or not, acting in a strange way. In addition to the safety tips given in the chapter on home safety to protect against invasion, there are further measures you can take. Positively identify callers before opening your doors and never allow any repairperson or salesperson to enter your home without first verifying their identification. Call their company if you have to. Be alert for any unusual or unexpected packages left at your home or workplace.

Have emergency telephone numbers programmed into *all* telephones you and your family use and clearly mark which button to push in case of emergency. If your telephone doesn't have a memory or speed dial feature, tape emergency numbers to it. Never rely solely on a cordless telephone. If the power to your home goes out or is intentionally cut, it won't work.

As soon as possible, tell a friend or loved one every detail of what's going on. This is especially important if you're married or have children. You shouldn't have to face this alone. Get emotional support from your friends and family, even if you don't tell each of them every detail. Let your neighbors and building superintendent or doorman know to watch for suspicious people. Know the whereabouts of all family members at all times and accompany your children to school or the bus stop.

At work, insist that the central receptionist handle all visitors and packages on your behalf. Alert your supervisor and co-workers to your concerns and the situation you're dealing with. Have your name removed from any reserved parking space. Travel to and from work each day at a different time and via a different route, staying alert for vehicles that appear to be following you. Vary your daily routine.

Above all, remember that it's not your fault. Taking precautions doesn't mean that you're letting a stalker control your life. A stalker changes your life, but you are still in control.

## Summary

Anyone can be a victim of stalking. Watch for early warning signs that a person might become obsessive. Be firm and if this doesn't work, ignore your stalker.

Inform the police of your problem and let them decide what steps to take. Keeping a journal of everything the stalker says and does can help them assess the risk.

Be especially vigilant, vary your routine and let friends and family know about your situation.

# Chapter 9:
# Identity Theft

In a small, blue-collar town, anything out of the ordinary stands out. So when residents noticed a group of young men walking through their neighborhood, knocking on doors and leaving, they took notice. It wasn't just because these men were strangers to the town. Their actions were suspicious.

One resident called the police, who set up surveillance along a neighborhood street. They soon realized what the group was doing.

Following a postal worker from house to house, one of the men walked up to each door and pretended to knock. Simultaneously, his other hand snaked into the mailbox beside the door and grabbed a fistful of mail. Then he returned to the street, passed the mail to an accomplice following in a car and walked to the next house.

Further investigations revealed that they were looking for one thing: pre-approved credit card applications. By submitting stolen applications with a changed address, these scam artists could receive credit cards they could use without paying a single bill. The delinquency, of course, would appear on the victim's record—a victim who, in many cases, would suffer the scorn of disbelieving collection agents some months later.

This story illustrates a crime called identity theft. Simply defined, identity theft is the act of stealing your good name to commit fraud.

For instance:

- When a criminal files for a car loan using your identification, it's identity theft.
- When he makes a purchase with your credit card number, it's identity theft.
- When he files for bankruptcy under your name, it's identity theft.

Identity theft is now the leading complaint of consumer fraud in North America, with an estimated 400,000–500,000 cases every year. Two out of five cases involve credit card fraud, followed closely by scams in which telephone or utility bill accounts are created in a person's name without that person's authorization. Related frauds include counterfeiting bank notes, travelers' checks, passports, health cards, Social Insurance/Security cards and driver's licenses.

Today, we work, shop and play in an electronic world where it's extremely easy for criminals to impersonate us. While most victims of identity theft eventually clear their names and recover the money they've lost, many suffer from the invasion of their privacy or damage to their credit records. However, you don't have to be a passive victim. By being Alert and Intrepid, you can greatly reduce the risk of having your identity stolen.

## Are you at risk for identity theft?

To determine your risk for having your identity stolen, check either Yes or No for each statement below.

| Risk Factor | Yes | No | |
|---|---|---|---|
| I carry my Social Insurance/Security card in my wallet. | ❑ | ❑ | 10 |

I receive several offers of pre-approved credit
every week. ............................................... ❑  ❑    5

I don't have either a locked, secure mailbox or a
P.O. box for incoming mail. ........................... ❑  ❑    5

I leave outgoing mail in an unlocked mailbox
or an out tray for pickup. ............................. ❑  ❑   10

I carry more than one credit card in my wallet........ ❑  ❑   10

I don't shred or tear up all banking and credit card
information (including pre-screened credit card
applications) when I throw it in the trash. ........... ❑  ❑   10

I give my Social Insurance/Security Number
(SIN/SSN) whenever I'm asked to, without asking
how that information will be used and safeguarded... ❑  ❑   10

I'm required to use my SIN/SSN at work or at
school as my employee or student ID. ................ ❑  ❑    5

I have my SIN/SSN printed on an employee badge
that I wear at work or in public. ...................... ❑  ❑   10

I have my home address and telephone number
printed on my personal checks. ....................... ❑  ❑    5

I give my SIN/SSN, credit card number or banking
information over the telephone or the Internet without
first verifying the identity of the caller and confirming
that the caller has a need for and right to the information... ❑  ❑   10

I perform financial transactions over the Internet
using a computer others can access. ................. ❑  ❑    5

I don't use a password to log on to my computer
at home or at work. ................................... ❑  ❑   10

I create passwords or personal identification numbers
that are easy for me to remember and easy for others
to guess (e.g., my birth date, my pet's name,
my nickname or any word in the dictionary). .......... ❑  ❑   10

I've set up my computer to automatically enter my user ID and password for websites I visit often. ..... ❑ ❑ 10

I send e-mail that contains personal or confidential information without encrypting the message. ......... ❑ ❑ 10

I don't occasionally request a copy of my credit report. ... ❑ ❑ 10

I don't follow up with billers if my monthly utility bills or credit card statements don't arrive when expected. ... ❑ ❑ 5

I'm listed in a *Who's Who* guide or an online directory that states I'm in a certain income bracket or a certain line of work. ..................................... ❑ ❑ 5

I don't believe that people will root around in my trash looking for financial information. ................ ❑ ❑ 10

Now, add up the points for each Yes response you checked. Your total number of points indicates your risk factor:

**100+ points:** You're at high risk. Becoming more security conscious can protect you from identity theft. Please start taking security precautions immediately.

**50-100 points:** Your odds of being victimized are about average; higher if you have good credit. Please start taking more security precautions immediately.

**0-50 points:** Congratulations. You're taking steps to protect your identity from theft. Tighten up security in the areas you've identified and don't let your guard down.

## How identity theft works

As you've seen, one way identity thieves operate is by stealing pre-approved credit card offers from the mail. They might also steal bank statements, credit card statements, telephone calling cards and tax information. Some will dig through your trash, looking for discarded documents. More elaborate tactics include searching public records or the Internet for information about you, obtaining your credit report by pretending to be a landlord or employer, or conspiring with store employees to obtain your personal information.

Once they have this information, identity thieves will commit fraud using your name. They might open a wireless telephone account to make long distance calls without having to pay the bill, or they might open a bank account in your name and write bad checks. They can counterfeit your checks, credit cards or debit cards, and use them to drain your legitimate account. They may even commit crimes or traffic violations and use falsified documents in your name for identification.

It's normally a long and difficult path to clear your record once your identity's been stolen and abused. It's much easier to take measures to guard your identity from being stolen in the first place. Next, you'll find out how.


Stating his name, "badge number" and "title" at the "Security and Fraud Department at Visa," a telephone caller told a credit card user that her card had been flagged for unusual activity. "Did you purchase an anti-telemarketing device for $497.99 from a marketing company in Arizona?" he asked.

"No," the consumer answered, with some concern.

"Then we'll be issuing a credit to your account," the caller said. "This is a company we've been watching for fraudulent activity and the charges range from $297 to $497, just under the $500 purchase pattern that flags most cards. Before your next statement, the credit will be sent to"—the caller then stated the consumer's address. "Is that correct?"

"Yes," she answered.

"I'll be starting a fraud investigation. If you have any questions, call the 1-800 number listed on the back of your card and ask for security. You'll need to refer to this control number"—the caller then stated a six-digit number. "Before we continue, I need to verify that you're in possession of the card."

The caller explained that there are three "security numbers" on the back of every credit card and that he needed her to read those numbers to him. After she did, the caller seemed satisfied that her card hadn't been lost or stolen. He thanked her and mentioned again that she should call Visa if she had any further concerns or questions.

In all likelihood, the caller had never anticipated that the consumer would call Visa with a question. When she did, the *real* security department at Visa told her that she'd been the target of a scam. A purchase of $497.99 had just been charged to her card.

The consumer was lucky to catch this scam early. She filed a report with the police and with Visa, and was able to clear the charge from the card. Many other consumers aren't so lucky and spend years fighting false charges or resolving damaged credit.

Frauds like this one work by hijacking normal social interactions. Since many people automatically defer to anyone who sounds, looks like or simply claims to be an official of some kind, scam artists often pose as authority figures. If someone approaches you in this manner, verify that person's identity or say you'll return the call. This consumer could have saved herself a lot of trouble by simply saying, "Thanks for telling me about this problem. I'll check my records, call Visa back and ask for you."

## Safeguard your personal information

The key to preventing your identity from being stolen is to safeguard your personal information, especially your credit card number and Social Insurance/Security Number. Your SIN/SSN is particularly vulnerable to theft, since it's the key to much of your personal, confidential information. However, since it's rare that you need to provide it, there's no need to carry your Social Insurance/Security card with you all the time. Store it in a locked cabinet or other secure location.

Disclose your SIN/SSN only to your employer and financial institution, and only when it's absolutely necessary. In Canada, your bank needs a SIN to open an RRSP, RESP, RIF or other tax incentive plan, but it doesn't need this information to open a checking or savings account. If you're asked for more personal identification than you feel is necessary, tactfully ask why it's required and what law demands that you provide the information. If you're given the choice to keep your personal information private, take that option. If not, find out how the information will be used and if it will be shared with others.

Keep any items containing personal information, such as charge receipts, insurance forms, checks, bank statements and credit offers, stored in a safe place. Shred or burn them when you no longer need them. Cut up expired credit cards. That way, criminals can't readily reassemble them. If you want to make things even harder, place half the shredded papers in one garbage bag and the other half in another.

## Category: ATM fraud

**How it works:** ATM crime takes many forms. The simplest is the thug who approaches customers and demands money. More sophisticated thieves, sometimes aided by a video camera, might watch an ATM customer enter her PIN number and later steal her card. In one recent scam, thieves installed magnetic card readers over the card slots of ATMs, created forgeries of cards that were inserted and used them to withdraw money.

**Warning signs:**

- Someone loitering around an ATM, especially if he sits in a car and gets out only when a customer arrives.
- Unauthorized withdrawals on your bank statement.

**Best defense:** Only use ATMs in well-lit, busy areas where unusual activity would be noticed. After business hours, the best choice is usually an ATM inside a supermarket, gas station or other public area. Watch for signs that ATM scam artists are at work. If an ATM is jammed or you see a handwritten note nearby, notify the bank or police immediately. One common scam is for thieves to purposefully jam the card slot. They then leave a note asking customers to call "security" at a given telephone number. Anyone who calls the number speaks to the scam artists, who request the caller's bank card number and PIN.

*Never* give your PIN to *anyone*. No one who works for the bank or its security division will ever ask for your PIN. If you want your spouse or older children to access your account, get an additional card for each person, each with a unique PIN. You can even set up withdrawal limits for each person, if you want to maintain control over your cash flow.

## Category: Check fraud

**How it works:** A criminal steals checks from your home, office or mail and forges your signature or alters what you've already written on the check. A common process is to remove ink from a check by washing it in a cleaning solution. Identity thieves can also print new checks in your name using a home computer and a printer.

**Warning signs:**

- You notice checks missing from your checkbook or your reserve supply.
- Outgoing mail containing check or bank information never reaches its destination.
- Billers call about overdue payments that you've mailed and they've never received.
- Incoming mail containing checks or bank information appears to have been tampered with.
- You spot unauthorized transactions on your bank statement.

**Best defense:** Don't carry more checks than you need and keep extras in a safe, secure place. Write checks using a pen that produces a thick, dark line and draw lines filling in the gaps before and after the dollar amount and the payee. This helps to prevent those fields from being modified.

Use checks with tamper-resistant security features designed to keep fraud artists from washing or counterfeiting your checks. Report any irregularities in your bank statement to your bank or financial institution immediately. Report mail theft or tampering to Canada Post or the United States Postal Service; this alone is a serious crime that can be prosecuted.

## Category: Credit card fraud

**How it works:** A thief may steal your card; someone may order a new credit card in your name by stealing a pre-approved application from your mailbox and requesting the card be sent to a different address; an unscrupulous sales clerk might make a duplicate copy of your credit card receipt or use a special device to read the card's magnetic strip; a scam artist posing as a bank official might ask you for your credit card number directly. The ways of defrauding with a credit card are as limitless as the criminal imagination.

**Warning signs:**
- Unauthorized charges appear on your credit card statement.
- You get a statement for a credit card you didn't request.
- Your mail appears to have been tampered with.
- Mail containing a new credit card or credit card statement doesn't arrive when expected.

**Best defense:** Contact the card issuer immediately if you receive a statement for a credit card you never requested or if you notice any unusual activity on your statement. Destroy all credit card receipts and statements you no longer need. Cut up old cards after they expire.

Pay attention to billing cycles and contact your creditors if their bills don't arrive on time. If you suspect that your credit card number is being used fraudulently, or if your card is stolen, take action immediately:

1) Call your creditors.
2) Call the major credit bureaus—Equifax, Experian and TransUnion—and ask that a fraud alert be placed on your file. Insist that they contact you if anyone applies for credit in your name.
3) Call the police.

To detect possible identity theft, order a copy of your credit report every few months from each of the credit bureaus listed above. Make certain that the report is accurate and contains only the activities you've authorized.

In the US and Canada, you can opt out of pre-approved credit card offers by calling 1-888-567-8688. Doing this protects you from some of the most common credit card scams. As always, preventing such scams is much easier than clearing your name after it's been stolen and abused.

## Summary

Protect your personal information, especially your Social Insurance/Security number, credit card numbers, and bank and PIN numbers. When asked to provide personal information, give the minimum required. Watch for the scams described in this chapter. And check your credit report regularly; that's the only way you'll know that your identity has been stolen.

If theft occurs, contact your creditors and the credit bureaus at once and file a police report. Don't submit to collection agency tactics; you are in the right. Be firm and relentless in restoring your good name.

Today, many of us work, play and communicate through the Internet. But since it's such a recent technology compared with telephones or the banking system, most people aren't aware of the risks inherent in a largely anonymous, global computer network. Identity theft is only one of them. In the next chapter, you'll learn about some others.

# Chapter 10:
# Computer and Internet Security

Even in the early days of the Internet, Michele was a veteran user of e-mail. She had an account at her university, which she used for keeping in touch with her classmates and professors.

She had received warnings about choosing a good, secure password and thought she'd chosen hers well. Her password was *grendel*, the name of the monster in the epic poem *Beowulf*. She didn't think anyone would ever guess it. To be even safer, she had checked it against an electronic dictionary to ensure it wasn't listed as an entry.

One day, Michele went to a comic book convention with a friend. They browsed through comics, discussed many topics and had some laughs. Only once did Michele make a comment about a character named Grendel, when she picked up a comic book with that character's name. It was an off-hand remark and she hadn't even been thinking about her e-mail password.

When she came home, Michele logged onto her e-mail account. To her surprise, she found an e-mail apparently from herself sitting in her inbox.

*Hi, Michele!* the e-mail read. *I can access your e-mail.*

After her initial panic, she realized that her friend had determined her password from that one casual comment and decided to play a prank on her. She immediately changed her password to something more secure and since then, she's been much more careful about the passwords she selects.

Michele doesn't use *grendel* as any of her passwords anymore, which is perhaps the only reason she'd let me include her story in this book. It was fortunate that her friend caught her insecure password, rather than someone with more malicious intentions. Someone else might have continued to read her e-mail and gather information while she continued to send and receive private e-mails, thinking they were secure.

In a sense, the Internet is lawless. Hidden behind a computer screen, scam artists and malicious hackers can commit fraud and steal your confidential information from halfway around the world. The traditional boundaries of law, country and personal identity blur and fade. And because of this, few of the Internet's outlaws are ever caught by authorities. The only way you can protect your data and your privacy is by creating your own defenses.

## Create passwords that are difficult for others to guess

Passwords are the only barriers to unauthorized access to most of your accounts, including e-mail and Internet banking. Once your passwords are compromised, there are no other measures to prevent malicious hackers from reading your e-mail or transferring funds from your account. This means you have to select your passwords carefully.

Many people select their passwords based on how easy they are to remember: a birth date, a pet's name or a favorite band. The problem is that a password that's easy for you to remember is usually also easy for someone else to guess, which defeats the purpose of having a password in the first place. When you're selecting a password, select it based on how hard it will be for someone else to guess. Never use any word in any language, because malicious hackers can run a program that tries every word in the dictionary to access your account. Instead, use a string of at least seven characters containing a combination of small and capital letters, numbers and punctuation marks.

| Insecure password | More secure password |
|:---:|:---:|
| max | MaX+4+2 |
| 081145 | bd0811DD |
| password | zg2a5*d^ |

One way of creating a password that's both secure and easy to remember is to abbreviate a sentence or phrase. For example, the sentence *In 1908, Lyndon B. Johnson was born* can be written as *i08LBJwb*, and the phrase *Tea for two and two for tea* can be written as *T42&24t*. If you select a phrase that has special significance to you, it'll be easy to remember.

It's important to select a password that you can easily remember; otherwise you might be tempted to write it down. In some offices, it's common to see lists of passwords written on sticky notes and pasted to computer monitors. By comparison, your mind is a much harder place for other people to get this information.

It's best to use a different password for each account you create and to change your passwords frequently. However, if you can't keep track of all your passwords, consider using a tiered system of three or four different passwords. For example, use one password for unsecured websites, another password for secure websites and e-mail, and a third password for your Internet banking. That way, if someone compromises a low-security password, your bank account is still safe.

In general, no one who administers your account will ever need to ask for your password. If they have the ability to administer your account, they also have the ability to access it. If you need to give a friend or colleague access to an account, consider changing the password temporarily, and change it back once she's done. That way, you're still the only one who knows your password.

## Protect against viruses, worms, Trojan horses and other nasty critters

Like a virus that infects you with a sore throat and makes you cough on other people, a computer virus attaches itself to a host program and spreads copies of itself when you run it. One by one, it'll infect your computer's files, and when you send an infected file to someone else, it'll infect files on that person's computer too. This means you should be cautious about running any new programs you download or receive, except for shrink-wrapped software from major software developers, which are generally safe. Don't open an e-mail attachment unless you're expecting it and know what it contains. If you're not sure, save it somewhere on your hard drive and run it through a virus scanner such as Norton Anti-Virus, McAfee VirusScan or Trend Micro's PC-cillin. Run any program you download from the Internet through your virus scanner too.

Worms are similar to viruses. Like viruses, worms spread from computer to computer, often leaving a path of destruction. The difference is that a virus requires human interaction, such as running a program, before it can spread. A worm doesn't; it takes advantage of security flaws inherent in your operating system. That means they're harder to guard against, without resorting to advanced precautions like setting up a firewall. The best way to prevent a worm infection is to keep your operating system and all your software up-to-date. A good anti-virus program can help too, since most will detect and eradicate worms.

The Trojan horse is another apt metaphor for describing a malicious computer program. The metaphor comes from a mythological breach of wartime security. During the siege of Troy, the Greeks built a huge, hollow wooden horse and filled it with some of their finest warriors. Then they left it at the gates of Troy and sailed away. Convinced that the horse was an offering of peace, the Trojans wheeled it inside their gates and celebrated their apparent victory with singing and wine. That night, the Greeks poured out of the wooden horse and massacred the Trojans.

In computing, a Trojan is a computer program that does a purported task while doing damage in the background. Unlike a virus, it has no need for stealth, since it operates under the cover of legitimacy. An electronic birthday card might play a pleasant melody while it's erasing files on your hard drive; a purported virus scanner might be sending your confidential information to a server over the Internet. However, a Trojan horse doesn't replicate on its own like a virus or a worm does. Someone has to send it to you or you have to download it from a disreputable website. To avoid Trojans, use only programs you know are legitimate.

Spyware is a generic term for software that collects information about you without your knowledge, usually for advertising purposes. It often installs itself without your consent, but sometimes it disguises itself as a legitimate application, much like a Trojan. Most spyware programs target the Windows operating system, often taking advantage of vulnerabilities in Internet Explorer. Alternative web browsers, such as Mozilla Firefox, tend to be more secure. If you suspect your computer has spyware installed, download and install Spybot Search & Destroy and Lavasoft's Ad-Aware. These free tools will search your computer for spyware programs and remove them.

Lisa was in love with Brett M., or at least she thought she was, as junior high students often do. Late one Friday night, she stayed up writing him a long e-mail expressing all her deepest feelings for him. She even wrote him a poem.

By the time Lisa clicked *Send*, she was exhausted. She turned off her computer and settled into bed for a long sleep, filled with pleasant dreams.

Halfway across town, Brett's sister was downloading music on the family computer. Brett had forgotten to log off his web mail account, so when Lisa's e-mail arrived, his sister saw it at once. She read through it quickly at first and then again slowly, giggling all the way. It was the funniest thing she'd read all week.

Brett's sister forwarded the e-mail to her own account. From there, she sent a copy to everyone in her address book. Before long, those people forwarded the e-mail to their friends as well. All it took was a few mouse clicks.

By the time Lisa woke up late the next morning, nearly everyone in grade eight was talking about her, her infatuation with Brett M. and her bad poetry.

## Anything sent via the Internet is potentially out of your control and potentially public

Anything sent or received over the Internet can easily be intercepted, since it has to be routed through numerous computers before reaching its final destination. Open wireless networks are particularly vulnerable to snooping, because anyone can park outside a home or office and connect to the network without a password. When you're simply browsing websites, this is rarely a problem, since no one takes great pains to acquire information that's already public. However, if you're sending confidential information, such as a credit card number, this information should be encrypted, or scrambled so it's not plainly readable.

If a website is secured through encryption, its URL will start with https:// rather than http:// and many browsers will display a small padlock icon. Send your credit card number through such sites *only* and take note if any security warnings pop up. Use your discretion if entering passwords and other sensitive information on sites that aren't secure. While it would be best for all such websites to offer encryption, this isn't always the case.

E-mail is not inherently secure, despite having a clearly defined sender and receiver. Each e-mail you send is routed through several computer systems and anyone with administrator-level access to any of the systems can read your e-mail. If you accidentally send e-mail to an invalid address, the e-mail and all its contents can end up in the mail administrator's inbox. Never write anything in an unencrypted e-mail that you wouldn't write on a postcard.

The best way to secure your e-mail when sending sensitive information is to encrypt it. The most common way of encrypting e-mail is through a tool called Pretty Good Privacy (PGP)— a modest name for a powerful program. Search the Internet for the free version and learn to use it. PGP can also positively identify a sender, which e-mail can't; the "From" header can easily be forged.

Sensitive files on your computer can also be encrypted with a tool like PGP. Then, if your computer is stolen or someone uses it without authorization, your sensitive information will be much harder to read.

Even after you delete files from the Recycling Bin or Trash, it's still possible to recover them. The information still resides on the disk or drive—you just can't see it. It's great to know this if you ever delete a file by accident (and you can afford data recovery services), but bad news if you want to keep your private information private. Programs like Eraser for Windows and Secure Delete for Mac OS allow you to delete a file securely by overwriting the information with zeroes or random data, the electronic equivalent of shredding.

## On the Web

If your web browser asks if you want to store your username and password for a website, click No, unless you're the only person with access to the computer. It's a convenient feature, but it essentially bypasses the security of a password.

When you shop online, don't save financial information such as credit card numbers at the websites you visit. Even a legitimate site can have a bad security model or a disgruntled employee who's unscrupulous and willing to commit fraud.

Be especially vigilant when using a public Internet terminal at a library or Internet café. Log out of any accounts you log onto and close the web browser when you're done. Don't perform Internet banking or other tasks that require tight security if you don't need to or if you doubt the computer's security. If the computer wasn't properly locked down, there's a small danger that someone has installed a keylogger, a program that records everything you type.

Be careful of what you disclose on the Internet. Once information's posted on the Internet, it's out of your control. Anyone can find it, copy it and redistribute it. Don't enter personal information into directories. If you have a website or a blog, consider using an alias instead of your real name. It's now common for prospective employers or inquisitive dates to search for your name on the Internet. Having years of private thoughts posted in public might not be in your best interest.

## Your computer isn't secure unless you maintain its security

Computer security experts often glibly state that the only secure computer is one that's locked in a safe and dropped to the bottom of the ocean. The physical security of your computer is often an overlooked aspect of computer security, perhaps because of its simplicity compared to network security. But even the best network protection can't stop someone who walks into an office, sits at a computer and quietly copies files to a disk or walks out with a hard drive in his briefcase.

The consequences of computer theft range from simple inconvenience to the loss of years of hard work or tightly guarded trade secrets. Laptop computers are a prime target for theft. Avoid carrying your laptop in a case made by any well-known manufacturer of laptop bags. Instead, consider putting the laptop in a padded sleeve and placing it inside a briefcase or backpack. Never let it out of your sight when using it in public and consider using a good cable lock to make it harder to steal. It's harder for a thief to walk away with a desktop tower because of its conspicuous size. However, if he only wants the information contained on the hard drive, he can remove that within minutes. Consider installing a computer alarm system on any computer that you use to store sensitive information.

Make regular backup copies of all your important data. Better yet, back up your entire system. You can copy files to an external hard drive or burn them to a CD or DVD. This will offer protection not only against security breaches, but also against hardware failure and your own mistakes. Store the backup media in a different location, in case there's a flood or break-in at the building housing your computer. Protect your backups as well as you protect your computer.

## Consumer fraud on the Internet

Exaggerated claims aren't always easy to spot, but if something sounds too good to be true, it's probably a scam. In a typical Internet fraud case, a product that you pay for doesn't arrive, or when it does, it's much different from the product that was advertised. When you're banking or shopping over the Internet, give your credit card number and other personal information only to companies you trust. If you don't know anything about the company, contact the Better Business Bureau (BBB) to find out if any complaints have been filed.

The auction site eBay has earned a good reputation from its buyers and sellers. Sellers who don't deliver as advertised are quickly maligned in public. Read the feedback on a seller before bidding and be cautious of sellers with very little feedback. While they may simply be new to the business, it's also possible they've recently created a new account to shake off bad feedback.

## People are the weakest link

Since ninety-three percent of face-to-face communication is through body language and tone of voice, the words comprising e-mail and web communication make up for only seven percent of normal communication. All the subtle cues that your intuition responds to are lost. This makes it much harder for you to detect insincerity over the Internet.

It's often said that the weakest link in computer security is *wetware*—in other words, humans. The latest technological advances can't stop a malicious hacker from transferring funds from your account if he sets up an official-looking web page asking for your banking information and you dutifully fill it out. Or he might call you, identifying himself as the manager of your company's IT department, and plainly ask for your password. Once you realize these scams exist, you can become more aware of how they work and less likely to fall prey to them.

A scam called "phishing" has recently been on the rise. Typically, the scam artist sends an alarming e-mail to consumers alerting them to a "problem" with their account. The e-mail includes a link to a website to "verify billing information", "re-activate your account" or "change an insecure password." That's the bait. If a consumer bites, she'll visit the scam artist's website, which is disguised as the legitimate one, and fill in private information. The scam artist can then use the information to gain access to the consumer's accounts, make purchases with the consumer's credit card number or otherwise steal her identity. To guard against phishing scams, be cautious about filling in personal information onto web pages linked from an e-mail, even if it looks official. Remember that on the Internet, authenticity is always in question.

Meeting someone from the Internet isn't much more dangerous than meeting someone in a bar or club. The complication is that many people misrepresent themselves on the Internet. How do you know that the new tennis partner you met online is actually a twenty-four-year-old medical student with a fondness for cats? There's only one way to know for certain, so when you're meet them for the first time, meet in a busy public location. Talking face-to-face is the only way your intuition can get a good sense of their character.

## Summary

One of the reasons the Internet is powerful is that it lets you connect to any other Internet-connected computer in the world. The problem is that the reverse is also true: any Internet-connected computer in the world can connect to yours. To prevent attacks and infections, update your operating system and your networking and Internet software regularly. Scan for viruses and spyware. Consider installing a firewall to limit unauthorized access to your computer; ask your Internet service provider or a computer-savvy friend if you need help. Watch for unusual activity, such as the send or receive lights on your cable modem or network card flashing for long periods when you're not doing anything on the Internet.

Be careful of what and whom you trust. Use encryption. Choose your passwords carefully. Make frequent backups and always prepare for the worst.

# Bibliography

Cialdini, R. *Influence: The Psychology of Persuasion.* New York: Quill, 1993.

de Becker, Gavin. *The Gift of Fear.* New York: Little, Brown & Co., 1997.

Elgin, S. H. *The Gentle Art of Verbal Self-Defense.* New York: Dorset, 1985.

Gilman, Rebecca. *Boy Gets Girl.* New York: Faber and Faber, 2000.

Grayson, B., Stein, M. "Attracting assault: victim's nonverbal cues." *Journal of Communication.* 1981, 31(1):68-75.

Mehrabian, A. *Silent Messages.* Belmont, CA: Wadsworth, 1971.

Luke Chao completed his Honors B.A. at the University of Toronto with a focus in English. A member of the National Guild of Hypnotists, he also helped to write *The Inner Power Series: Abundance for Life, Love and Money.*

Lloyd Vaughan completed a twenty-six year career with a major Canadian police service, specializing in criminal intelligence operations and VIP security. He has traveled extensively, conducting international organized crime investigations and lecturing both to police and civilians on investigative techniques and safety. He has also protected and provided security intelligence for heads of state, government officials, movie stars and members of three royal families. He lives with his wife in rural Ontario and is the co-owner of LTD & Associates Inc., an international investigative and security consulting company.
Website: www.ltdsecurity.com